Inside A Woman

Revealing Her Longings, Pain, and the Journey to Love

by Jane Hansen
with Carol Greenwood

Aglow Publications

A Ministry of Women's Aglow Fellowship, Int'l.
P.O. Box 1548
Lynnwood, WA 98046-1548
USA

Cover design by David Marty

Women's Aglow Fellowship, International is a non-denominational organization of Christian women. Our mission is to lead women to Jesus Christ and provide opportunity for Christian women to grow in their faith and minister to others.

Aglow Publications is the publishing ministry of Women's Aglow Fellowship, Int'l. Our publications are used to help women find a personal relationship with Jesus Christ, to enhance growth in their Christian experience, and to help them recognize their roles and relationship according to scripture.

For more information about Women's Aglow Fellowship, please write to Women's Aglow Fellowship, Int'l., P.O. Box 1548, Lynnwood, WA 98046-1548, USA, or call (206) 775-7282.

ISBN 1-56616-000-6

DEDICATION

This book is dedicated to my dear husband Howard who has walked with me on the journey to love. Without Howard's release and support of me in the ministry God has called me to, this book would not have been possible.

Acknowledgments

Although this is the story of one woman, it could never have been written without the love and encouragement of many, many people.

Two people head the list—my pastor and his wife, Dick and Marilyn Williamson. I will be eternally grateful for their love, their counsel, and the truth they have so faithfully imparted to my life through their ministry. In one chapter of this book, I have referred to myself as a "wounded bird." This is an apt description of my condition when I arrived on their doorstep.

God used them to bring me out of myself, out of my hiddenness, out of my pain, into the light of his truth. The help I received through their biblical counseling has been nothing less than the radical, life-giving heart surgery that is crucial to a changed life. Thank you, Dick and Marilyn, for giving yourselves so selflessly to me and to the Body of Christ.

My heart is filled with gratitude, also, as I think of my husband Howard. His support and belief in me—and this book—has never faltered. His willingness to be known and his desire to help others is a great tribute to the work of God in his life.

I am grateful to God for the wonderful gifts he has given me in our children, Jeff, Lisa, and Scott. Their love and their continued encouragement, not only through this project, but in the way they have so graciously released me to do what God had called me to, is indeed a precious expression of their love.

It is not an easy process to feel another person's feelings, hear her heart, and then communicate that message. My friend, Carol Greenwood, has done just that for me. Her faithfulness and commitment have helped make this book a reality. She is to be applauded for the hours and hours of work she has given: hours of reading and interpreting handwritten notes, hours of listening with her heart, hours of writing and rewriting so as to carefully express all that is inside this woman.

Thank you, Carol, for your belief in this project and your willingness to set your hand to the plow and not look back. Thank you, Dick Greenwood, for your willingness to eat TV dinners, do your own laundry, and burn the midnight oil with Carol. Thank you, Gail Greenwood, for the hours of inputting on the computer and even sacrificing days of work to help.

There are so many who have carried the vision for this book and undergirded us with prayer: Susan Goodnight, VP of Publications, who has stood on the sidelines cheering us on, praying us through hard places; Doris Eaker, VP of Prayer Ministry, who served as my assistant for so many years and who along with friends, Pat Gaines and Christa Murrow, believed in this message and encouraged the project from the start; Karen Anderson, Acquisitions Editor, for her incredible support and superb editing; JoAnne Sekowsky, for the hours of copy editing; Karen Husband, a computer whiz who gave valuable expertise; Deena Wilson, Leadership Training Coordinator, for her valuable ideas and input; Betty Ringer for the use of her Florida home as a place to write.

Thank you to so very many loving, encouraging, praying friends . . . too numerous to mention.

And last, but certainly not least, a big thank you to Dee Fink, my assistant, and Cheryl Morgan, my secretary, who have undertaken superhuman work loads on my behalf that this book might be published. And Lorene Carlson, Executive Vice President, who has picked up the responsibility of overseeing the Aglow international headquarters to free me to give myself more fully to this project, as well as other avenues the Lord seems to be opening before me.

As I reflect on all the precious, godly people the God has so lovingly placed in my life, I am truly humbled and awed by his concern for me.

Thank you, Jesus.

Jane Hansen
Edmonds, Washington, USA
June, 1992

Contents

Foreword

"Give her of the fruit of her hands, and let her own works praise her in the gates" (Prov. 31:31 KJV).

We have been privileged to be Jane's friends and have watched the changes in her life as the Lord ministered to her words of faith, truth, and encouragement. We have seen the person God created her to be coming forth. This happened as she gave up the protection of the person she had been using to cover up what she saw as her inadequacies.

We believe that Jesus used the Holy Spirit to uncover the inside woman of Jane Hansen so that she could become an able minister to other women as she serves as International President of Women's Aglow.

Vulnerability means to be "open to be wounded"—no self-protection. Jane has risked this, letting you see her heart, being transparent before you, to help you. She believes that what leaves the heart reaches the heart.

We believe that Jane's desire for you as you read this book is that you take it into your heart for your help.

Jane's pastor and his wife,
Dick and Marilyn Williamson

Foreword

I took Jane to the airport early this morning. She was off on one of many weekends of speaking to groups of ladies throughout the United States and overseas.

She called me this evening from Dallas Airport. Because of an intense storm, the flight had been redirected, finally arriving in Dallas after a five-hour delay. She would not arrive at her destination until after midnight. She asked me to pray for her so she would have peace and rest. I did.

This evening I drove to downtown Edmonds, parked the car, and took a walk on the lovely street along the Puget Sound. It was windless, the water was calm, and the sun was beginning to set. A balmy evening. Beautiful. At the end of the street I sat on a bench and viewed the sight that both Jane and I admire so much. I felt lonely—I wished Jane were with me. Yet I knew she was doing God's will as a speaker and teacher.

As I sat there in peace and quiet, tears came to my eyes. I felt sad, yet it was a good feeling, because I felt love for not only Jane but for the Father. Now I can feel love and show emotion. I did not feel this way years ago. I now have a Father that I can talk with anytime.

Jane was traveling, yet I felt her near me, and I thanked God for her and the help she has given me through these years. Had I not married Jane 33 years ago, I would never have been in the place I am now.

I now have the love of Jesus in my heart. I can now have tears in my eyes and feel emotion. I can now have feelings. I can now forgive and be forgiven. I can now have peace in my life.

God has been good to Jane and me. Jane has a heart for all people. She is a giving, generous, and caring person.

What she has written in this book has taken many hours of burning the midnight oil so that what is said will help someone out there who reads it.

What was written is the truth, and I admire her for telling the whole story.

I thank God for Dick and Marilyn Williamson and their love, understanding, and friendship. I honor Jane today with a heart full of love for her. Thank you, Jane, for putting up with me and a lot of bad behavior during these many years. Thanks for your understanding and, most of all, thanks for your undying love for me through it all. You are a great lady.

May God bless you always, and I love you very, very much.

Your husband,
Howard

Introduction

I love the way God's Word so clearly shows life as it was really lived by those He came to save. It is all there: the good and the bad, the mountaintops and the valleys, the triumphs and the failures . . . the truth of the process. Their struggles and their victories encourage us onward in our own journey through life.

God is so willing for it all to be seen; the pain of His people was not hidden, nor were their fears or insecurities covered over. God is so willing to let it all be seen, that we may be encouraged and helped on toward His purpose in our lives.

Writing this book has not been easy for me. I have struggled with the fear of being known. Yet because of the help I have received, I felt that my struggles and victories might also encourage you, the sisters I have so come to love.

In Dr. Larry Crabb's book *Inside Out* he states, "The church needs leaders who can involve themselves in other people's lives with the joy of integrity and transparency . . . willing to be deeply known for the sake of helping others."[1]

He goes on to say, "God wants to change good disciples into powerfully loving servants who leave an indelible mark on people they touch."[2]

That is my prayer, that my life, all of it, can somehow touch yours and together we can walk that journey towards love. This would fulfill the prayer of Jesus that the world would see our love and come to know the Father.

15

1
...
Pain in the Little Red House

The real estate agent eased his car to a stop alongside the white picket fence. "Well, folks, here we are. The second house on our list today and is it ever a charmer." It was the fall of 1959 and my husband Howard and I were hunting for our first house in a neighborhood close to Seattle's Northgate shopping center.

The agent placed his left arm on the steering wheel as he turned toward Howard and said with man-to-man intimacy, "Your wife's going to love this little dollhouse." As he spoke, he rolled his eyes as if to say he understood the mystery of a woman's tastes. Then, glancing toward me in the back seat, he resumed his professional demeanor. "Mrs. Hansen, ahh . . . would you mind if I just called you Jane?"

I don't remember answering him. My mind was not on the

formalities of agent/client protocol. I was so transfixed by the sight in front of me that my mouth must have fallen open.

Inside a little white gate and up a short walk stood my picture perfect house—the kind I'd yearned for ever since I was a preacher's kid growing up in church parsonages.

Amazingly, this little red house looked like a double of a favorite house from my childhood that we passed by every Sunday on our way to church in Akron, Ohio. I was bathed in nostalgia as I stared. I had found a long lost friend.

"This little gem just came on the market, Jane." The real estate agent grinned at me, then turned back to open the car door. "Come on folks, let's take the grand tour." He slid out and slammed his door behind him.

Before Howard could open the passenger door, I leaned forward, put my hand on his shoulder and blurted, "Howie, it does look good." Howard nodded as he carefully swung three-year-old Jeff from his lap onto the parking strip. He reached back to help me out, then boosted the excited tot up high on his broad shoulders and I felt a spark of pride. I loved the natural way Howard took charge of his little family.

We followed the realtor through the gate and up the walk as he continued his patter. "You and Howard are wise to get settled before your baby comes. There's probably not a better home in the north end for your little family. This one has two bedrooms, big kitchen, nice fireplace, and a family room for the kids." He paused on the doorstep, looking for some kind of response from me, but I was still too excited to say anything.

We walked into the living room and the men stopped in front of the fireplace. "Take a look at this mirror work, Howard." Howard eased Jeff off his shoulders and onto the floor.

As I wandered off to explore the rest of the house, the

realtor's voice followed me, "Wait till you see the apple tree in the backyard, Jane." I heard the men resume their conversation, but all I could think about was the first chance of my life to choose paint colors, wallpaper, and furniture.

Jeff and I found the bedrooms and opened closet doors. As we walked down the hall, I talked to my tow-headed son as if he were my decorating consultant. "Let's see, honey, I'll use lavender and white in Mommy's and Daddy's room, repaint the little bedroom for you and our new baby, and hang white curtains and green towels in the bathroom."

"New baby can sleep with me, Mommy." Jeff offered as he flashed an innocent smile. "I take care of him." Wrinkling his freckled nose, he was an irresistible target for a motherly kiss.

"Do you have any idea how I much I love you, honey?" I leaned over impulsively and put my lips against his upturned cheek. Straightening up, I wrapped my hand around his little one and walked him toward the kitchen.

As Jeff scooted ahead, I paused under the archway to the kitchen. Looking at the inviting kitchen and out to the garden beyond the large windows was like being tossed into the multicolored freshness of a spring morning while hearing my favorite symphony. A rush of energy flooded me as all of my senses were engaged at once.

I felt exhilarated with the sensation of the new life flutter-kicking within me, and now with another wonderful sense of expectancy.

I could bloom in a place like this, I thought. This is what I've always longed for, a home of my own.

A NEW START

At that moment, I could not have told you why I felt such a need for a new start in a new place. My longing for a new home was the immediate answer but, as I would discover later, the yearning went way beyond satisfying the life's desire of a new homemaker.

The apartment we lived in on Queen Anne Hill was certainly not undesirable. But I wanted to feel the freedom of ownership. I wanted to turn loose all my creative home-making energy to personalize our surroundings. Decorating, painting, sewing—I loved to create warm, inviting rooms.

"Mommy, look at the little doors!" Jeff's voice brought me back from my reverie, but before I could react he ran to my side. When his pudgy fingers tugged at my skirt, I couldn't resist his enthusiasm. Together, we ran to the long row of cupboards under the counter and I squatted down with him. We giggled as we took turns opening and shutting each door.

As the afternoon sun splashed through the large windows, diffusing warmth and light throughout the room, this joy-filled moment between mother and son struck me as heaven sent.

"Your wife like to bake?" It was as if the realtor read my mind as he ushered Howard into the kitchen. I had mentally baked an apple pie using apples from the backyard tree.

"Yeah, Jane's a great cook," Howard responded matter-of-factly.

While they talked, I fingered the long white counter tops, my creative juices flowing.

Finally, I couldn't contain myself. My words tumbled out as I broke into their discussion. "Howie, can't you just see this kitchen with red checkered curtains? I can sew them in a snap. It won't cost much to buy a red canister set and it will really pull this room together, don't you think?"

The agent laughed at my outburst as Howard answered, "Sure, whatever you want to do." Then he headed toward the back door to inspect the backyard. I followed him out and caught my breath at what I saw. Ablaze with watermelon-colored poppies and flower beds exploding with color, the backyard looked like a park. Surrounded by the white picket fence, complete with the advertised apple tree, the sight was far more beautiful than I glimpsed through the window.

Years later, I would drive by this home again and see only a small, nondescript house on a quiet street, but then—at that moment—standing close to Howard, it felt like a mansion to me.

The realtor cleared his throat in the silence. "I think your wife's found her dream house, Howard." Eager to close the sale, he began to turn back into the house. "Why don't we all head back to my office, have some coffee, and talk about making an offer?"

Before Howard could move, I grabbed his hand and squeezed it hard. "It's perfect, Howie." Howard stood silent for a moment and I barely breathed. "Let's do it," he said. And we did.

We bought the little red house that sunny, blue-sky Seattle day. Within six weeks, we moved into our first home.

IMPERFECT REALITY

Perfect. Perfect. Perfect. The words sang in my heart like a lullaby during those early nights in the red house. I'd lie in bed next to Howard, mentally rocking myself to sleep with my perpetual fantasy: Life will be perfect for our little family with this dream home to wrap around them. I could almost hear the bluebirds of happiness chirping out reservations for nest space in our apple tree.

However, within weeks of our moving in, I wondered if the bluebirds had migrated south. What was wrong? I had

21

everything I wanted. I should be happy. But happiness did not move in with our furniture and boxes as I thought it would. In fact, something else was creeping in like an unwelcome fog around the edges of my heart as I sewed curtains and painted bedrooms.

HAPPINESS IS . . .

It may be hard to believe from the perspective of today's fast-paced, success-oriented society, but in those years, I wasn't interested in pursuing a career, prestige, or financial success. In fact, it never occurred to me.

I'd been raised in a pastor's modest home in the midwest, and my aspirations reflected the simple, down-to-earth growing up days of the '40s and '50s. Anytime anyone asked me what I wanted out of life, I gave them my standard answer: "Give me a home, children, and a husband who loves me and I'll live happily ever after."

I came by this love of home and hearth naturally. I remember as a little girl of four or five, stepping onto the yellow linoleum floor of my great–grandmother's kitchen in rural Ohio, closing my eyes, and inhaling the intoxicating aroma of whole-wheat bread baking in the oven.

Later, as I watched her bend over her sideboard to roll out piecrust, it was as if everything in that cozy kitchen sang out, "Home is wonderful. It is warm, secure, and safe."

My mother followed in this homemaking tradition. In every parsonage we called home, she plunged in to shape a comfortable and attractive haven for our family. Her creativity seemed inexhaustible—even in some of the aesthetically challenging parsonages.

Somehow, womanhood really "took" with me. It wasn't only that I grew up in an era where women's roles were more closely related to the home than they are today. I wasn't emulating the apron-clad mom on the '50s TV shows. As a little girl I spent hours dressing dolls and having tea parties. During my teen years, I loved fixing up my room and learning to bake and cook.

To this day, I believe it is a God-given desire in a woman to fashion a home and to lovingly fill it with warmth and beauty for all who enter.

Understandably, my hopes for our life in the little red house were high.

OUT OF REACH

That "something" I'd felt inside myself just after we moved in increased when I began to notice a growing aloofness in Howard. As a newly appointed Vice-President of Marketing and Sales for a west coast tour company, he was feeling the pressure as a young executive on the rise in the burgeoning travel industry.

After work, when he pulled into the driveway, I'd rush to the door to let him in, eager to hear about his day and share mine with him. When I'd ask him how his day went, he'd give me a perfunctory "Okay," or "Just great," then brush my cheek with a quick peck and walk past me into the bedroom or kitchen.

I couldn't figure out why this talkative, breezy guy, the one with whom conversation was always so easy in our dating days, was suddenly not talking.

This was the man who used to entertain me with his nonstop stories and jokes. This was the man who, during our courtship, would twirl me around and plant a big kiss on my cheek and beam me a dazzling smile. Now, within a few brief months, he had become more than untypically quiet. He was distant.

More than once I pursued him with words, on into dinner, just trying to connect. I tried to find the old Howie

I knew, the upbeat, happy-go-lucky guy I married. But all my conversational gambits dropped at my feet like unopened parachutes.

As the weeks wore on, I began to feel a quiet desperation for that closeness. Like someone lost in a desert of need, I looked to Howard as my well, certain it held the elusive water that would satisfy my thirst for affirmation and affection. If only I could bring up the bucket. . . . But I couldn't even turn the crank.

I couldn't have known then what even Howard didn't recognize: that he was hurting from the unnamed pain in his childhood. Now, with his responsibilities as a husband, father, and sole provider of a growing household, he suffered silently from anxiety and a sense of growing inadequacy.

But I couldn't see that. So, I tried harder.

ALONE TOGETHER

In one sense, our little red house was my beginning place. At last I could indulge my domestic creativity. At last I could create a home.

I spent my days baking Howard's favorite things, sewing for our baby who was expected in less than three months, and working in our garden. One thing I never doubted about myself was my competency to create a warm domestic atmosphere.

But I began to feel increasingly incompetent in the area of our personal relationship. Somehow, in spite of all my efforts, the one thing I really wanted eluded me: intimacy—a warm, loving, connection with my husband.

One night shortly after we moved in, I edged over to Howard's side of the bed and extended my arm to massage his back. "Howie, we're going to be happy in this house, aren't we?" I moved my hand up to stroke his shoulder and neck with my fingertips.

Howard stiffened. He pulled his arms snugly to his side and mumbled, "We could have knocked down the price, but basically we did okay."

I leaned over and planted a little kiss on his back. "Thanks, Howie, this home means a lot to me." But there was no response from my husband except a quiet, "Hey, I'm tired . . . okay?"

His words weren't harsh but they puzzled me. I couldn't understand this new distancing. It was as if a heavy curtain had dropped between us. Howard was on one side and I was on the other, feeling abandoned.

It was spring and we'd been in the red house five months now, but instead of growing closer together, we were drifting apart. The thoughts gnawed at my mind. Was it me? Had I done something wrong? One question I barely dared ask myself: Am I terribly ugly as a pregnant woman?

Most of the time, I felt too humiliated to bring up the subject of "us" again. But once, when I mustered my courage to ask Howard one more time why he was aloof, he looked at me blankly for several seconds. Then he said quietly, "Jane . . . I don't know."

A MOMENT OF JOY

Howard's actions may have mystified me about our relationship but I was sure about one thing with him. He really loved children. His reaction at seeing his new baby daughter was wonderfully spontaneous.

In the early morning hours of May 18, 1960, our baby Lisa arrived and for the first two days, Howard wore a nonstop, full-faced grin, and my spirits lifted with his. "Jane, she is so cute," he said.

Fathers didn't have the easy hospital access to newborns in those days that they have now. Even so, Howard's delight was obvious. Everyday he walked with me down to the nursery, pressed his face against the window, fixed his gaze on our little daughter, and shook his head in wonderment.

"Look at her sleeping like an angel." He'd pause to cast his eye on the current crop of newborns snug in their cribs. "She's really the prettiest one here." He may have been slightly prejudiced, but then so was I.

BEGINNING AGAIN

We drove home with baby Lisa in my arms and Jeff in the back seat. Would this miracle of childbirth mean a new start for Howard and me? My face flushed with anticipation as we rounded the corner of our street and caught sight of our little red house.

Home. How I loved all I wanted it to mean. Maybe we would be set now. Two children, Howard's job going well. I made up my mind to be positive. It's going to go well for us, I thought. I just know it.

That self-generated hope propelled me with new energy to cope with the late night feedings and all the extra work involved with a new baby. I even pushed myself to exercise so I'd get back into shape, convinced that real change was—if not immediate—just around the corner for Howard and me. I would make it happen.

As Howard's job responsibilities increased, his travel schedule kept pace. Sometimes he'd be gone for a few days. At other times, he'd be gone for more than a week. Meanwhile, with one young child and a new baby to handle, I really missed him.

Lisa was barely two months old when he left on a three-week trip to Alaska.

One day, shortly before he was due back, I found myself going under with the same old feelings of abandonment until an idea hit me. Why not surprise Howard with a special welcome home dinner and evening with just the two of us? It had been eons since we'd taken time to cuddle up on the sofa and talk.

From then on, planning Howard's surprise consumed me. Although our budget was tight, I thought I could even manage a new dress.

The little pink sundress with spaghetti straps in the store window was perfect. The saleslady brought it to the dressing room in my pre-baby size. Now was the moment I would know for sure. Had all my exercise and fifteen-pound weight loss paid off? As I zipped myself up past the waistline, I knew it had. I nearly cheered right there in the dressing room.

The day before Howard was due back in town, preparing his favorite foods took priority. My perfect schedule for the next day included time for a bath for me during the kids' naps and an early bedtime.

I was convinced again that this was going to be the evening when I would turn things around in our relationship, when that wonderful spark would be back between us, just like in our courting days.

Mercifully, the day Howard was expected home, Jeff and Lisa went down for their naps without a whimper and I luxuriated in a bubble bath and got a chance to wash and set my hair.

Just before dinner, I bathed and dressed the kids and left them playing quietly in the bedroom while I fixed my hair. As I pulled on my new dress and put on my makeup, the result I saw in the mirror pleased me.

Howard's car pulled into the driveway and I smoothed the waistline of the dress before I went to the door. There he was, my husband, the man I loved, looking road-tired as he wearily carried his bags into the living room. He gave me a quick kiss before Jeff pounced on him with a whoop. "Daddy!"

As Howard took a shower and unpacked in the bedroom, I managed somehow to get Jeff into bed with a promise that "Daddy will play with you tomorrow night."

I had just put the plates on the table and lit the candles when Howard came into the kitchen wearing slacks and a sport shirt. Hungrily, out of the corner of my eye, I looked for a smile, a wink, some recognition as I walked around the kitchen in my pink dress. I wanted to know, not only that my dress looked good, but that I was special to him.

As we sat down, his eyes avoided mine. Instead, they passed over the pot roast in front of him and slid over to the homemade apple pie on the counter. Then, after his first bite, the compliments flowed. But they weren't about me or my dress. "Wow, Jane, restaurant food will never compare to your cooking."

Just before dinner I had been ravenous, but that night I toyed with my food as we talked about his trip, the flight, the yard, and finally the weather. This is just like it's always been, I thought. I could feel disappointment rising within me as tangible as mercury in a thermometer.

Howard finished his pie, pushed his chair back from the table, and headed out to the front yard. My heart sank to the floor as I sat with my eyes riveted to the skirt of my new dress. I swallowed hard and felt a lump form in my throat.

I wanted to scream, "Don't you even see me?" But I didn't. I just listened to the flap of the screen door as it shut behind him.

When I finally stood up from the table, I sensed life draining out of me. My head whirled.

I looked at the water goblets in my hand as I carried them numbly to the sink. I'm as empty as you are, I thought as I slipped them into the dishpan.

DARK WATERS

Many nights in the weeks that followed, I reached out my hand in the dark for some reassuring touch but drew back when Howard turned away from me. Sometimes I felt like I was swimming the English Channel in mid-December. Chilled to the bone marrow, I wondered if I'd reach shore without dying of hypothermia.

Shore. Where was shore?

Even now, I was still certain I knew. It was a home where a husband looked up over his evening newspaper and, in a voice exuding caring, said, "Jane, do you know how much I love you?" It was a place where my deepest needs would be filled to overflowing with unconditional love, where my inner emptiness would dissipate under the tender touch of my husband.

I thought I'd be safe forever inside that little red house with Jeff, our new baby, Lisa, and most of all, Howard.

But I was wrong.

Ironically, it was here, where I expected to be the happiest, that I encountered the strongest, most gnawing pain of my young life. Somehow I had to find a way out of such darkness.

2
...
The Family Tree

Emotional scars and the accompanying pain don't just materialize out of vapor, they come from somewhere. Like rings in a cross section of a giant redwood tree, they are telling records of the traumas and storms in our lives.

David Seamands, in his book *Healing of Damaged Emotions* points us to this example from nature.

In most of the parks the naturalists can show you a cross section of a great tree they have cut, and point out that the rings of the tree reveal the developmental history, year by year. Here's a ring that represents a year when there was a terrible drought. Here are a couple of rings from years when there was too much

31

rain. Here's where the tree was struck by lightning. Here are some normal years of growth. This ring shows a forest fire that almost destroyed the tree. Here's another of savage blight and disease. All this lies embedded in the heart of the tree, representing the autobiography of its growth.[1]

"And that's the way it is with us," continues Seamands, "Just a few minutes beneath the protective bark, the concealing, protective mask, are the recorded rings of our lives."[2]

THE PERFECT FAMILY

No one is born into a perfect family. In the human realm, we are all deprived of the kind of unconditional love we crave that only God provides. Sin has left its poisonous bite, its insidious scars on every generation. Parents don't love perfectly and children don't always perceive their love clearly.

When parents do not, or cannot, spend time developing loving relationships, or where there is turmoil in the home, the simple truth is, children are affected.

Hardly without exception, they will grow up feeling emotional pain in place of the security and love they need. In a word, they will feel deprived.

Have you ever felt that way as an adult? As if you're not worth others' attention or love? As if they really shouldn't take time to bother with you?

I remember my fiftieth birthday when some friends of ours took Howard and me out to dinner. When we got home, I took one innocent step forward into our darkened family room when suddenly the lights flicked on and a roomful of friends chorused, "Surprise!"

As I gazed at their delighted faces, I felt an instant

crosscurrent of emotions: Joy and gratitude for their loving affirmation of me, yes, but I confess I also felt a twinge of embarrassment. It was the very thing I didn't deserve. Yet, it was the very thing I needed.

These feelings of not being worth anyone's time or effort haunted me most of my life. I can't pinpoint the moment they crept in, but I do know that they appeared at an early age. And I learned early to cover them over.

MY STORY

Like the redwood tree that hides its history inside its healthy looking bark and branches, the outside indicators of my childhood were all tidily in place: Two capable parents, food to eat, a house to live in, and clothes to wear.

I may have looked like a quiet little girl bouncing through life with plaid ribbons tied at the end of my pigtails, but the real me, the one unknown to anyone but God, was aching inside. Never mind the ribbons in my hair, I had a larger ribbon knotted around my heart. It read: Hurting child.

Poor innocent child. Who's responsible? Who's to blame?

Isn't that the question our litigious society would ask? It's the same question the disciples asked Jesus about the man born blind: "Who sinned, this man or his parents, that he should be born blind?" (John 9:2 NAS). Where can we point the accusing finger?

BLAMING OR HEALING?

Someone wisely said, "While you blame, your wounds can't heal."

Clearly, my parents—and Howard's—made mistakes. Clearly, every other parent in the world has made and will make mistakes, myself included.

But blaming parents is not on my agenda. Looking at reality is.

Our impressionable growing-up years can hold invaluable clues to understanding the people we are today. If there have been hurts, as there were in my life—and surely most everyone else's—the truth is that these cannot be healed if they are denied, or if others are not forgiven.

THE HEALING BACKWARD LOOK

An honest look backward at the family I grew up in has helped me identify some of the hidden rings of my life.

Meet my father, Tom Williamson. If you saw his picture in the family photo album, you'd be drawn to this handsome young man from Belfast, Ireland, with dark wavy hair and snapping blue eyes. If by some technological marvel, you could hear him talk or sing, you would be enchanted by his quick Irish wit and his soaring tenor voice.

Dad wanted to be an opera singer and with this goal in mind, he studied music in school. His family saw the potential he had and encouraged him. But voice and music lessons had to be paid for. That couldn't come from an already stretched budget supporting a family of six. Dad had to earn a living, and as many young men in Belfast did at that time, he went to work in the shipyards.

A LIFE-CHANGING MEETING

Then, in the early 1920s, something happened that forever changed Tom Williamson's life.

Revival swept through Northern Ireland. W.P. Nicholson, a well known evangelist of the time, preached powerful messages each night in the Newington Presbyterian Church. Word spread fast and the hungry crowds packed the pews. Shipyard workers came by the droves, directly from work,

34

in order to find a seat. They came carrying newspapers to fold around themselves so their dirty work clothes wouldn't stain the pews.

Each night, when Reverend Nicholson gave the altar call, he did something unheard of in the staid Presbyterian Church of that day. He asked those accepting Christ to stand and say, "Mr. Nicholson, I take Jesus Christ as my Savior."

On April 2, 1922, Dad could no longer sit in his seat. Wild horses couldn't have held him back. He leapt to his feet and professed that he would "take Jesus."

And Jesus "took" my father.

Dad was never the same. His heart was instantly captured by the Savior and inflamed with His love. What is more, he couldn't keep quiet about it. Dad must have told us his testimony a hundred times. And every time he told it, his eyes filled with tears when he repeated the unforgettable moment when, as he put it, "For the first time in my life I heard the Gospel."

Shortly after his conversion, Dad left Ireland with his father, to look into the possibility of life in the United States. The family was to follow. But when Dad's mother became ill, his father returned to Belfast. Tom stayed on and settled in Flint, Michigan.

Dad was a modest man, not given to seeking the adulation of others, yet he was unembarrassed about his reputation as "the fiery Irish evangelist." We were told and retold stories of how he stopped on the way home from work to preach on the street corners of Flint. They are rich memories for me.

When Dad was unable to dismiss the Lord's call to ministry, he made a hard decision. He chose to lay aside his lifelong dream of a musical career and became an ordained pastor in the Christian and Missionary Alliance denomination. His beginning pastorate was in Mount Vernon, a small town near Columbus, Ohio.

That first Sunday from his pulpit, Dad could not help but notice the talented church pianist, Mystel Burson. He thought her playing was extraordinary and she was beautiful as well, with a mane of reddish gold hair and a modest manner.

Mystel became his wife and my mother. Her early pictures show her as a sparkling, fresh-faced young woman. When she and Dad met, Mother was preparing to enroll in the prestigious Eastman School of Music in Rochester, New York. She wanted to pursue a lifelong goal as a concert pianist.

OPPOSITES ATTRACT

Their romance didn't blossom overnight, but almost. These two musically gifted, bright young people who loved God couldn't help but be attracted to each other. Tom, the fun loving, witty Irishman and Mystel, beautiful and talented, though prone to worry, married and settled down in Mount Vernon, Ohio.

Early in their marriage, it became apparent that Tom and Mystel had two very different temperaments: An optimist had married a pessimist.

Dad, a man of passion, immersed himself in whatever he was doing. An unquenchable fire seemed to burn within him. He loved life and being around people, singing and telling his zany jokes.

Mother took life seriously. She could be pleasantly social whenever the occasion demanded it, but she was never naturally gregarious like Dad. She simply could not comprehend her husband's easy-going Irish personality, his lightheartedness, and his penchant for telling what she considered "corny" stories.

On top of that, her parents frequently bemoaned the fact that their talented daughter forsook a promising musical career to marry a "poor preacher." Mother struggled often with her insecurities and anxiety.

When my brother, Jimmy, was born, he won my parents' hearts immediately. Four years later, it was my turn.

Six weeks after I was born, Dad took a position as head of the music department at the Bible Training Institute in Nyack, New York. We lived there for two years, then moved to Akron, Ohio, where he became pastor of another Christian and Missionary Alliance Church.

The Akron photos depict us as one happy pastor's family, smiling and seeming to thrive on the activities of a demanding ministry: My blond, sensitive older brother, Jimmy, and I appear in pictures as scrubbed and dressed with care. "When you came," my mother used to tell me, "we knew then we had the perfect family, a boy and a girl."

Perfect?

My memories of myself during this time are meager. I felt alone much of the time, lost in the busyness swirling around me, isolated from the hub of all my parents' ministry activities.

Dad was well thought of in the denomination in Akron and gained further recognition as a music director as well as preacher, who led traveling choirs and quartets and gave public concerts.

Mother, insecure as always, but ever his faithful accompanist, trooped right along with him.

My mother's attention was directed at me every morning as I sat on a stool in the kitchen and she brushed and braided my hair. It was a time for us to talk and for me to tell her briefly about what was happening in school before she started her chores and other activities.

Family vacations were nonexistent. Even summers gave no respite. Instead of taking days to camp or picnic like other families, we crisscrossed the country in the car so Dad and Mother could preach and sing at all the summer conferences.

There was no time for Jimmy and me to do the things kids do on hot, lazy days. We couldn't run down a path in the park with our arms flying from our sides; we couldn't squeal at the top of our lungs as we were pushed in a swing. There was no time to twirl around in the backyard and drop like dead men at our parents' feet.

What I remember most was sitting. We sat in the car, we sat in the pew, we sat in the social hall after the meetings.

THE FROZEN IMAGE

Cameras only capture an image frozen in time. They can't reproduce truth on film. I discovered later that there was much more to the picture than the handsome pastoral couple with the well-behaved children. Just as the tree ring that shows blighted years covered by the bark, underneath our scrubbed family facade, the Williamson family was showing signs of cracking. Not having enough time to spend together as a family was taking its toll. Especially on me.

A HUG-ON-THE-RUN

"Daddy, could you help me with my homework?"

I didn't scream or yell for his attention, but when I needed Dad, I'd try snagging him right after dinner, before he flew out the door to church.

"Let's see your arithmetic book, honey." For a few idyllic moments, I would squeeze up to Dad's side, tablet and pencil in hand, eager to hand him my book and paper, but even more desirous of having his attention.

"Oops, you can't subtract six from seventy-four without borrowing." He'd wink at me and shake his head. "Jane, you're my little apple blossom, do you know that?" I loved those tender moments when he called me apple blossom, but they were never long enough. He was the apple of *my* eye, my knight in shining armor. I adored him.

When Dad glanced at his watch and got up from the chair, I felt guilty for always wanting to prolong our time together. It was what I wanted more than anything else, to feel close to my daddy for just a little bit longer. Couldn't I have more than a hug-on-the-run? I asked myself.

"Sorry, honey, I can't take any more time now. I love you." He'd grab me for a quick squeeze and dash off.

A kind of subdued longing engulfed me as I watched my dad and mother disappear out the door, calling out their instructions to the baby-sitter as they rushed down the front steps to Bible study, choir practice, or prayer meeting.

I wanted to talk with someone who had time to listen. I wanted a hug that didn't feel like something you grabbed for at a convenience store as you dashed in and out. But I sensed that their lives were filled with important things to do, more important than I was. But it wasn't until later that I came to see why.

How could I tell anyone how I felt then? This was the man I idolized. My dad preached sermons that kept people on the edge of their seats. This man had famous friends such as Bible scholar, Dr. A.W. Tozer and Dr. V. Raymond Edman, president of Wheaton College. Everyone loved Tom Williamson.

Mother's gifted homemaking did not keep her from being nervous about the parsonage being "open for inspection," with people stopping by unannounced with hand-me-down clothes or vegetables from their gardens. During those visits, Mother's directions to Jimmy and me were explicit: "Mind your manners. Remember, you must set a good example."

After all, we were the pastor's children, obligated under God, to reflect his good name.

I sensed this restrictiveness in our "be good, look good" fishbowl life and knew there wasn't room for me to complain or cry.

When Dad was home, he frequently secluded himself in his study to read, prepare sermons, or write music. My ten-year-old head accepted it, but more than once I crawled into bed with a sad heart and a mind full of questions without answers. Doesn't Daddy really love me? Doesn't he want to spend time with me?

Then I'd picture Dad up in the pulpit, the place I saw him the most, preaching about the mysteries of God in eloquent language, and I'd fall asleep with his shining face etched in my mind. It wasn't the same as cuddling up on his lap, but it was the best I had.

GOODBYE AKRON, HELLO GLENDALE

The church in Akron grew under Dad's ministry both numerically and spiritually and both Mother and Dad forged many strong friendships in the community.

However, a large church in southern California asked Dad to come, and, finally, he decided that the Lord was speaking to him to "go West."

But how we hated to leave Akron! As an eleven-year-old who came to Akron at age two, it was the only home I remembered. My brother, Jimmy, and I were comfortably settled in school, doing well with our studies. I had made a few close friends, and Jimmy had a thriving circle of teenage companions.

For pastors' families, moving goes with the territory, and our family could not escape this ritual. But when it came time to say goodbye to Akron, five hundred people turned out at a farewell reception for us. Dad, Mom, Jimmy, and I stood side-by-side as every person filed past to give us their tearful goodbyes.

TOUGH GOING

We arrived in Glendale only to discover this would be a difficult season in our lives.

Many of the promises made to my dad went unfulfilled. Nothing seemed to work out the way we expected. The first year was particularly painful. We couldn't seem to make friends like we did in Ohio, and we were homesick for those we left behind. Many lonely evenings, the four of us walked the streets in silence, holding hands, and wondering if our hearts would ever mend.

Of all of us, Jimmy was hit the hardest. At fifteen, he struggled to make his way into established peer groups, but he couldn't penetrate them, either at school or with the young people at church.

Somehow this fresh-scrubbed, sensitive boy from the midwest just didn't fit in. His inability to make the transition caused Jimmy to look elsewhere for acceptance. Unfortunately, kids whose influence was anything but positive, accepted him, and soon drinking, smoking, and staying out late became his way of life.

Jimmy's behavior added pain to this already stressful time in our family. The move from Akron to California, now was weighted with a new crisis point.

My parents were struggling. Dad was involved in activities from morning to night. In order to keep up with Dad, Mother's pace stepped up. She added to her crowded days by entertaining parishioners often. She fed and housed visiting pastors and missionaries. Always aware that someone from church could pop in at anytime, she drove herself to keep the house immaculate.

More and more, their innate differences in temperament emerged as friction points in my parents' marriage. The result was an uneasy tension and behavior that resulted in one snapping at the other, returned by hurt looks or quiet withdrawal.

A NEW DANGER

Stress, by its nature, doesn't idle in neutral. Not only was our home fueled with it, it was accelerating.

During this vulnerable period in my parents' relationship, a woman in the congregation began to make deliberate, flattering overtures toward Dad.

In today's world, this incident would be labeled a friendship. It certainly was, in no sense of the word, an affair. This mild flirtation resulted in no clandestine meetings. What it amounted to were some casual conversations before church meetings or after choir practice. But in her witty manner, using a moment here and there, this woman affirmed Dad's preaching and musical talent in a way that briefly turned his head.

Mother gradually grew aware of the woman's actions. She already felt insecure about Dad's love for her, and these incidents served to underscore her doubts and weaken their relationship even further.

A full blown marital crisis erupted under our roof.

Instead of snapping followed by silence, tears and angry accusations ricocheted through the house. The worst part was that I was in the middle, caught in the crossfire of two hurting people that I loved.

CAUGHT IN THE CROSSFIRE

"Do you think Dad loves me?" Mother turned to me, a pre-teenager, for her emotional solace. Then, in a voice filled with hurt, she would say, "Nobody really cares about me."

In his way, Dad also turned to me as he made asides about mother's nervousness and constant fretting.

If it wasn't their own relationship they talked about to me, it was Jimmy and their anguish over his behavior. Jimmy, in turn, confided in me his frustration with parents who "don't have time for me. All they want is for me to march to their own little drumbeat."

Typical of most families in the midst of relational dysfunction, all three family members elected a go-between—me.

As a twelve-year-old girl I hated this emotional battle-ground. I was caught in the middle, waving a small white handkerchief of truce in every direction, but nobody seemed to notice.

A POCKET OF GRACE

Looking back now, I see a pocket of grace in the midst of that whirlwind, a tender touch of the Lord to a little girl longing for her parents' love, yet caught between two hurting adults.

My Aunt Ina and Uncle Bill and their daughter, June, the cheeriest Irish folk in the world, came to stay with us while they looked for a home. In the midst of the pervading gloom and doom in our household, they greeted me each morning with an uplifting word, a hug, or sometimes a lilting Irish folk song. It was as if someone had thrown open the door to let in the sunshine with a fresh spring breeze.

I got real hugs from Aunt Ina and Uncle Bill and for a few short months, they accepted me, stabilized me, and touched my life in a deeply meaningful way.

REPENTANCE AND GRACE

Every storm has its fallout. Downed branches. Power outages. Overflowing gullies. Eventually something tangible had to give in our home, too. Mother was on the verge of a nervous breakdown, the culmination of a long period of undealt with issues in her life. Dad realized her fragile condition and came to his senses. He finally saw his foolish behavior for what it was: selfish, destructive, sinful.

Broken and deeply repentant, he went to the district superintendent to resign from the ministry.

"Tom, I cannot let you do that." The superintendent was adamant. "The call of God on your life is so recognizable, I would be a fool to let you go."

Instead of leaving the ministry, Dad resigned from the Glendale church and served as a traveling speaker within the denomination, while Mother, Jimmy and I returned to Ohio for several months.

It was to be a healing time for our family, with reunions that were frequent and sweet.

THE UNSEEN FALLOUT

And me? I didn't realize the toll these years took on me.

I do remember one day shortly before my thirteenth birthday, I stood in front of the hall mirror in the parsonage in Glendale and studied myself. There I was in hand-me-down clothes, with my childhood braids gone and in their place, a frizzy perm. I looked straight at the reflected Jane and thought, Who are you, little girl? You have borrowed clothes, a borrowed house, and borrowed parents. No wonder no one hugs you.

Most psychologists know now that even very young children are incredibly perceptive about picking up signs of stress in their parents' marriage. All I know was that I felt absolutely trapped, pulled to be loyal to both parents and to a brother I dearly loved.

On one hand, I wanted to set everything right; on the other hand, I wanted desperately for all the hurt and anger to go away forever. I felt responsible, as if I were the only stable one in this storm.

What I wanted was a family but I couldn't fix all their problems.

But one day, alone on my bed, I made a quiet decision of my own, one that was in my control. If I couldn't fix them, I could fix it for myself. The results of that decision affected me emotionally for years:

I swore to myself that no man would ever hurt me the way Dad hurt my mother.

3
...

Making Choices

The crisis in southern California was over. The storm that rocked our home for nearly two years passed, sweeping with it the debris of misunderstanding. The winds of adversity, which had battered Mother's and Dad's marriage so strongly, subsided.

In the calm that followed, their new love and commitment began to take root within the rich soil of understanding and acceptance.

Now back in Ohio, Jimmy, now nineteen, lived with us only briefly in Ohio before he joined the Air Force and headed for Korea.

It was a new era.

Dad's growing reputation as a preacher of the Word made him a sought-after speaker. One admiring colleague

47

told him, "When I hear you preach, Tom, my preaching sounds like the squeaking of a gate."

Word of Dad's preaching quickly spread to the west coast. We'd been back in Ohio only a year when he accepted a call to a church in Berkeley, California. Once more, the moving truck pulled up to our house. Once more, Mother packed and labeled our furniture and household goods.

A NEW MISSION

Because this was a new mission church, there was no parsonage. Mother, Dad, and I moved in with a family in the congregation for three months until a parsonage became available to us.

Their home was lovely and the family, gracious to us. Carla, their daughter, was three years older than I and owned a closet full of clothes. Sharing her room showed me a world of cashmere sweaters, wool pleated skirts, Spalding white buck shoes—everything that was "in" for girls at Berkeley High School in the '50s.

But for me, opening her closet door was like opening Pandora's box: All my old feelings of personal deficiency came rushing out of hibernation. I continually compared myself to Carla, whom, I believed, had everything I needed to be accepted: clothes, looks, sophistication, popularity.

She rated at the top of the scale. But not me. In my mind, I utterly lacked those ingredients; I was still that little girl standing before the hall mirror with a frizzy perm, dressed in hand-me-downs.

Later, when we moved into the parsonage, I took an after school job at Hinks Department Store. I bought myself the coveted Spalding shoes and several downy soft cashmeres. It felt so good to wear something new and all my own. These were not hand-me-downs.

Yet, even beautiful clothes could not fill the emptiness inside me.

A NEW CHANCE IN COLLEGE

After graduation from Berkeley High School, I enrolled in what was then Seattle Pacific College, a small, Christian liberal arts school nestled alongside the Lake Union Ship Canal. It was my first introduction to Seattle, a beautiful setting, and, for me, a socially freeing environment.

For the first time in my life, I was comfortable with my contemporaries, young people reared with the same values I was. In high school, because of all the things I couldn't do as Pastor Williamson's daughter, I'd always been the outsider. In Seattle, in a Christian college, I felt I could freely enter into all school activities.

I blossomed. Soon I was participating in many aspects of campus social life as well as sports.

My freshman year flew by. However, by the end of the year, I was uncertain of my academic direction and concerned about the financial burden my schooling placed on my parents and on another family who shared the costs. I returned to Berkeley.

In downtown Oakland, I found a job as a secretary in an office and continued to live at home. I was bringing home a regular paycheck as a young working woman. My life was stabilizing again.

Then one day, without warning, I was thrown into a situation that raised sheer terror in my heart.

A WORD FROM GOD?

One morning while Dad was having his usual coffee at the local bakery, a young man joined him at his table and soon plunged into a conversation about his faith. After that, the two often met to discuss spiritual matters. Sometimes they'd go for a walk together, sometimes Dad invited him home.

When I met this young man, I felt oddly uncomfortable around him. I was put off by the way he seemed absorbed with his own spirituality.

One day, out of the blue, he called me at home, insisting that God told him I was to be his wife. Stunned, I couldn't believe what I was hearing. I hadn't the slightest romantic interest in him. I was eighteen years old with my life ahead of me and the whole marriage idea gripped me with fear.

That evening, I went immediately to Dad for counsel, fully confident he'd come to my rescue.

"Dad, this is really scary. What should I do?" I remember looking into Dad's eyes, confident that he would immediately label the idea as preposterous and usher this man out of our house and our lives.

Incredibly, Dad hesitated.

He felt he couldn't risk intervening in case he might somehow miss God's leading. So he simply stepped back and let the pronouncement stand as if it were possibly God's will.

I panicked. Here was the man I so admired and looked up to, the one who represented God to me, the one I counted on for spiritual wisdom, *and he didn't step forward to counsel or advise me*.

I interpreted his silence to mean one thing: that God himself had acquiesced to this pronouncement. I might soon be signed over as a pawn in what felt like an arranged marriage.

At that time, my idea of God was that of a God-with-a-big-stick; a distant, aloof, corrective Creator who made arbitrary decisions about human life. If I didn't like it, too bad. After all, who could argue with God?

A suffocating panic gripped me. This directive seemed

to hold some irreversible countdown on my life. After all, I had no vote.

As the months went on, my panic grew. It was as if I were marching toward a cliff I knew was there, but no one yelled a warning. I was walking to the brink alone, in a thick silence.

Then, one day, a new young man started attending our small church. Everyone seemed drawn to him. I liked his twinkling brown eyes and ready smile, but now I realize I also was drawn to him as a person ready to fall off a cliff is drawn to the hero on a white horse who rides to the rescue with a strong rope.

Within a few short months of our meeting, the young man with the ready smile and I were married.

As you can well imagine, we were two young people ill-prepared to enter into marriage, but we did—for all the wrong reasons. It was a brief, but disastrous event. Two years later, we separated, then divorced.

Here I was, a pastor's daughter, raised in an evangelical Christian home. I'd spent most of my life trying to please my parents and now, with one wrong choice, a feeling of absolute failure engulfed me.

Pain and grief washed over me in waves. One day, I'd feel as if I could lift up my head, face the world, and walk tall again. On another day, I'd be swamped by a thunderous onslaught of guilt. This was never a turn I thought my life would take. I felt permanently marked.

It would take years and the cleansing blood of Jesus to heal me.

STARTING AGAIN

I was single again.

I was a woman with no rings gleaming on her finger but one bright ray of sunshine glowed in my dark world—my blond, blue-eyed Jeff. Four months old, he was the light of my life.

Where was God in all my confusion? I know now what I didn't know then: He was close at hand. The Lord was right there, weeping over my sin and pain, yearning to draw me to Himself. He was reaching out to me, His arms open and His hands extending unconditional love and forgiveness. But in my perception then, He seemed disinterested in the hurts and wounds of people.

I related to God then much as I did to my earthly father: He had time for everyone else, but not for me. As far as I was concerned, I was on my own.

FACING REALITY

Overnight, the realities of my life contained some very practical issues. I was now a single mother who needed an apartment, a job, and someone to care for her baby while she worked. A tall order, it seemed, but I was determined to make my own way and not be a burden to my parents. After all, I reasoned, I'd already let them down enough.

Fortunately, jobs were plentiful and I was able to find what I needed: loving care for Jeff, a small apartment, and a position with a travel agency close by. Life went on. I was busy and finances were tight, but I was making it . . . barely.

I'd been at the travel agency a month or so when I started having coffee and an occasional lunch with Genevieve, a gracious young Australian girl. As a busy single mother with little time for a social life, I relished opportunities for stimulating adult conversation. Genevieve and her husband were avid travelers. They'd work for awhile in one place and then move on to see more of the world.

Although I'd crisscrossed the U.S. with Mother and Dad, I'd never traveled overseas, so listening to Genevieve's stories was much like watching a fascinating special on *National Geographic*, narrated with a delightful Australian accent.

One morning, in an off-handed way, Genevieve mentioned her boss, Howard Hansen, who'd been spending a lot of time out of town on business. "I'm eager to have you meet him, Jane. He's so easy to get to know, you'd really enjoy him."

I appreciated Genevieve's intent, but meeting men wasn't on my agenda; as far as I was concerned, I'd be single the rest of my life. So mindful was I of my marriage failure that, if any man had seriously approached me at that time, I would have run in the other direction.

But as the months passed, others in the agency dropped comments about Howard, and Genevieve remained quietly persistent. "Wait till you meet Howie, Jane. You're going to love him." By now, of course, I was curious.

One day, Genevieve brought a tall, broad-shouldered, blue-eyed blond with a California suntan to my desk. "Jane, I want you to meet Howard Hansen." From our first meeting, we had a relaxed rapport. Soon we were chatting comfortably at the water cooler, then at coffee, and occasionally over lunch.

At the office or at lunch I couldn't help but notice how others also warmed to Howard. He seemed to be the life of the party, with time to joke or chat with everyone. This blond Dane with the sunny disposition and warm, affectionate nature began to warm my heart in spite of myself.

Then one morning, Howard stopped by my desk and invited me to dinner.

As Howard and I began seeing each other, "dinner out" became a home-cooked meal at my apartment. For a mother of a little one who had to pay for a baby-sitter, going out anywhere was a real luxury. Even though a meal at home, with Howard across from me at the table and Jeff between us in his high chair, was hardly a romantic evening, it seemed easy and natural.

Howard and I took turns helping Jeff cut his meat, then wiping off his sticky hands. During the moments in between, we squeezed in our own adult conversation.

Howard's gentle caring manner, especially toward Jeff, comforted me in an indescribable way. Before dinner, the two of them would laugh and giggle on the floor, sometimes tossing a ball or playing peek-a-boo. It was like two bear cubs, Howard performing with a tender abandon, and Jeff playing with exuberant delight.

What a contrast with Dad, I thought. Dad, who was the center of attention outside the home, sought solitude to study or listen to symphony music, as soon as he walked through the parsonage doors. At the time, I felt he was closing himself off from us.

Hearing Howard's laughter inside my little apartment gave me a real lift, while other signs of his caring for us melted my heart.

One winter evening after we'd picked up Jeff from the baby-sitter's and walked into my apartment, Howard reached in ahead of me to switch on the lights. Nothing happened.

I knew immediately that it wasn't a burned out light bulb and was glad that the darkness hid my embarrassment. After an awkward few seconds I managed to mumble, "Howard, there's a problem. . . . I've been waiting for my next pay check before I mailed in the light bill."

Without a sign of reproach, Howard set my groceries on the kitchen counter, turned on his heel and was out the door, calling after me, "Be back in half an hour, Jane." And he was, carrying with him the paid-up receipt for the light bill in his hand.

Mix all his qualities together and it's easy to see why I fell in love with this man who cared for me and genuinely cared for my son. Ten years older than I, Howard was settled in a good job with a promising future and he was a faithful churchgoer.

We were married in February, 1959, and off for a brief honeymoon in Carmel, California.

BRINGING IN THE BAGGAGE

Picture the honeymoon couple: Blissfully, they return home from their first few days together as husband and wife. He carries her over the threshold and gently sets her down. They embrace and spend a long moment gazing into each other's eyes. Finally the bride whispers sweetly, "Darling, we need to bring in the suitcases."

The groom dashes to the car, and deposits the contents in the front hall, saying with pride, "I guess we're ready to start our married life. I just brought in the baggage."

Little does any honeymoon couple know at the time, that when they put their suitcases down in the hall, they've also carried their emotional baggage right in the door with them. This baggage doesn't fill the car trunk and it doesn't contain jazzy sport outfits, beautiful lingerie, or glamorous evening wear. In fact, none of it is pretty to look at, especially once it's out of the bag and draped across its owner.

Howard and I both brought emotional baggage into our marriage. This baggage had been left open since our childhoods. Piece by piece, item by item, our first hurts and emotional pain went into a little cardboard suitcase. Through our teen years, in duffle bags, we continued to pack in more hurts, fears, pain, false perceptions of ourselves and others. Finally, we added layers of self-protective strategies. The bags filled up.

Elaborate coping mechanisms, masks to cover pain, layers to hide flaws—they all went in. Years later, when we were long entrenched in behavior patterns and beliefs that directed our lives, even the facade of sophisticated soft-sided luggage couldn't disguise the sinful contents.

HOWARD'S STORY

Howard, like I, was reared in a pastor's family. The youngest of three boys, he grew up in the midwest. If you were to open the Hansen photo album, you'd see Howard's dad, a first generation Danish immigrant. A man of personal strength, he knew what he believed and didn't mind telling others.

A sincere, born-again believer, Howard's father was, nevertheless, exacting with his boys. His parenting was not untypical for an era when such a premium was put on hard work and being obedient. He was a strict disciplinarian, and Howard remembers he was one who spoke harshly when obedience was not forthcoming.

"If I didn't obey my father," Howard said, "I would be spanked or disciplined in some other way. That was something I really feared. As a 'preacher's kid,' I knew I had to be good."

Howard's mother was the understanding nurturer. Howard grinned with delight when he recalled the way she warmly cared for him. "She was a quiet, gentle, very loving woman," he said. "That's probably why I hung around the kitchen so much. I liked being with her." She always seemed to have time for him. Whether it was to read to him, help with his homework, or talk with him in the warm glow of their kitchen, "I could always feel her love and sense her acceptance of me."

To this day, his mother's words of unqualified praise echo in his memory. Once, as a fourteen-year-old, Howard took a washing machine motor and rigged it up to power his bike. He drove his new invention—something no one in town had seen—past her viewing spot on their Montana parsonage porch and basked in her applause. "Howard, you've done a wonderful job."

As much as his mother's praise meant to him, Howard secretly longed inside for some word of approval or acknowledgment from his dad.

"Like many men, my dad was unable to show much outward affection or give warm words of affirmation to his sons," Howard says now. "He deeply cared for us and he would do anything for my mother, but affirmation from the head of the household, in an era of absolute obedience, was not considered a virtue." Yet, back then, Howard's sensitive boy's heart longed for open, honest conversation.

The Hansen family's day began with devotions at breakfast, with everyone, including Tippy the dog, in his appointed spot. Howard still remembers wanting to eat quickly and leave the table because the whole process seemed so regimented. "We'd only talk about surface kinds of things, the weather, the church, sports. No one ever talked about how he felt, whether he was mad, sad, or glad."

At school, Howard shrank from the day that one of the kids would ask what his dad did for a living. "I'd just mumble, 'minister.' " That word told them that Howard couldn't go to movies or join them in some of their activities. Since it was too awkward to be one of the boys, often he spent time with the men of the church who took a lively interest in him and his projects.

Later in life, whenever Howard went to visit his dad as an adult, he was immediately escorted downtown to be shown off to the barber, the grocer, and the rest of his dad's friends having coffee at the bakery.

In his head, the adult Howard knew his dad was proud

of him. Otherwise, he wouldn't be so eager to display his adult son. "But my emotional baggage was there to tell me otherwise," said Howard. "My heart still carried the stamp of the childhood perception that I wasn't important as a person, just as a performer."

Howard and I both learned to be performers, to play a role, in our childhoods. It was part of the baggage we brought with us into the little red house.

A PHYSICAL REACTION

After Howard's homecoming from his Alaska trip, life for us continued in emotional isolation. My pink dress stayed out of sight in the back of the closet. I didn't need a physical reminder of my pain when I had a biting memory of it.

But soon another pain, a debilitating physical pain struck, one I could not pass off.

Howard glanced at me with worry in his face. "Better check with the doctor, Jane." He headed out the door for an early morning meeting at his office. "You've been doubled over with that pain for two weeks now." He was right. All my home remedies weren't touching my excruciating stomach ache.

The doctor's words hit hard. "Mrs. Hansen, your test results are back. I'm sorry to tell you that your severe abdominal pain is caused by a bleeding ulcer." He paused to let the news sink in. "An ulcer is nothing to fool around with, and a bleeding ulcer. . . ." The doctor reached for his prescription pad and sighed. "I know you have Lisa and Jeff to take care of, but somehow you're going to have to try to reduce the stress in your life. Why don't you and your husband get away from the kids for a weekend? A break would do you good."

It was my turn to sigh. Had this been the '90s with a

greater concern for the interrrelatedness of physical and emotional well-being, the doctor might have looked me square in the eye and said, "What's going on in your life?" But at that time, he assumed I was another tired young mother.

"You need to fill this immediately." He placed the slip of paper in my outstretched hand. "I want you started on medication by this afternoon." Then, with a look at my resigned expression, he put a hand on my arm. "Be encouraged, Mrs. Hansen. We see good results in a matter of a few weeks with this treatment and a bland diet."

As I put the kids in the car and drove to the drugstore, the doctor's words continued to ring in my ears: "You've got to reduce the stress in your life."

Easy for you to say, Doctor. Have you ever had two little ones, a tight budget, a yard to keep up, and a husband who seems as distant as the man in the moon? My defensiveness surprised me. But I quickly rationalized that feeling. This is a pretty big assignment for one woman, I told myself.

Back at home, I tucked Lisa and Jeff into bed. I lingered in the room, listening to the soft sounds of their breathing and shut the door carefully, amazed at how quickly kids fall asleep. Today, I was grateful; we all needed a break.

As I wandered into the living room, I kicked off my shoes and sank into the big overstuffed chair. Weary from the hectic morning, my body sagged with relief. But my mind stayed in motion. Like a dog with a bone, I wanted to keep chewing on this stress issue.

Quickly, I discarded the idea that running the house and taking care of children was that stressful. Homemaking energized me, satisfied me. And the kids? They were a handful, but wonderfully fulfilling.

Just then, a sharp pain jabbed me in the stomach with an

intensity I couldn't ignore. Neither could I ignore the moment of truth. Tears filled my eyes as I sat there on the sofa. My stomach may be hurting, I thought, but my heart is hurting more. I just can't let my marriage fail. . . . I knew all along that only one person could fix my excruciating heartache, and that was Howard.

THE WOUNDED BIRD

I got up and wandered to the kitchen window. Outside, in the thicket of the juniper hedge bordering the picket fence, a tiny sparrow seemed caught on something, moving only his head in sharp, jerking turns. Curious, I opened the kitchen door, walked to the side of the house and inched quietly along the hedge.

What was wrong? Why did he stay put when he was in such obvious terror? Why didn't he fly from his prickly hideout?

Up close, I found my answer. His feathers, rumpled and mashed on his right side, parted just enough to expose his drooping wing hanging limply from his body. No wonder this little sparrow couldn't fly, he was wounded—too wounded to do the very thing he was created to do.

In many ways, I felt like that wounded bird, wedged into my own emotional hiding place. I felt restrained from entering into life fully, as I knew it was intended. Instead, I set myself up for a cycle of disappointment over and over. I didn't see it then, but I worked hard to attract Howard's attention and, when I didn't get what I needed, I quietly retreated into myself. The place where I withdrew felt akin to a cold, damp cave. Here, nothing could reach me.

Where was God? Surely the God who encouraged the little children to come to Him and who made the little girl spoken of in the Gospel of Luke rise from her deathbed, had created me to soar.

This same God who, I know now, had a plan for my life, also had infinite patience. Not put off by my flailing in the darkness, He could—and He did—wait until I came to the end of myself.

But I wasn't there yet.

ONLY TEMPORARY SILENCE

Busyness has a way of temporarily silencing pain. To take the edge off, I plunged into community and church activities.

Howard and I joined a Lutheran church in our neighborhood. Even though my father had pastored another denomination, I was willing to join Howard in the church tradition he'd known all his life.

Churches always need volunteers and there were plenty of slots for my help. I assisted at women's circle, luncheons, and receptions and was rewarded with good feelings of accomplishment, new friends to share with and, most important, a distraction.

FROM RED TO YELLOW

We'd spent four years in our little red house. Jeff was "going on eight," and it was time for him and four-year-old Lisa to have separate bedrooms. I was pregnant with our third baby when we sold "Little Red" and bought what we called "the yellow house on the hill." Here, two months after we moved in, our son Scott, was born.

With a beautiful new baby and a new neighborhood, my spirits lifted. Karen and Jim, the couple next door, immediately reached out to us. Their home was filled with beautiful paintings, interesting art pieces as well as stimulating conversation. My world, so centered in home and family, expanded, thanks to these two.

Karen was ten years older than I and an accomplished

artist. She shared her decorating savvy and fashion tips
with me, stretching my horizons and helping me to grow
in confidence as a woman. How I enjoyed that kind of
nurturing friendship!

Howard continued to do well in the travel business and
we lived in the yellow house only a few months before he
received a promotion along with news of a transfer.

As regional sales manager for the tour company, he was
assigned to a branch office in the Los Angeles area. Howard
flew down to work in Los Angeles almost immediately. I
was thrilled that he continued to be rewarded for his
ability and hard work, but it meant another separation. I
was to wait with the children in Seattle until the house was
sold before we could join him.

TO CALIFORNIA WITH A PROMISE

Sometimes Howard flew home on weekends, ready for
a break from the pressure of a new job. I greeted him at the
door, ravenous for adult conversation after spending all
my time as a temporary single parent. As usual, I didn't
know how to get him to open up.

"What's the new office like, Howie?"

He'd toss out a quick reply and head for the lawn
mower.

I knew by now that my hopes, high when he came home
on Friday afternoon, would plummet to the ground by
Sunday night.

I needed a permanent solution for my growing emotional agony but I'd gotten to the place where I was too
needy, too hurting, too close to view my situation objectively. In the emotional poverty of my marriage, I blamed
myself and desperately searched for Howard's affirmation.

Howard pushed the lawn mower back and forth, back
and forth across the lawn and my insides knew that motion.

But mine was done in in my mind. I cut a wide swath in one direction for my personal insufficiencies. Then, turning in the opposite direction, I mowed my way back toward the side that affirmed me as a woman of value. One of these days, I thought, I'm going to mow myself down.

Shortly before the last time he returned to California, Howard walked into our bedroom to pack his bag. With the house sold, the children and I were to fly down to California as soon as the final papers were signed.

"Need anything from the laundry room?" I called.

"Nope. Got everything I need in the drawers here, Jane."

I stood in the bedroom door and stared at my husband, memorizing his big build and blond hair, everything I loved about him.

"I'm going to miss you, Howie."

The sox were on the bed in little rolls and his face and hands were concentrated on gathering them together to put into his suitcase. He never looked up.

A few minutes later, Howard walked into the kitchen where I was peeling apples for the kids' snack. I could feel a burning in my stomach; my ulcer was acting up again.

"Time to leave for the airport," he said breezily. "I'm glad the kids are over their colds." He leaned against the counter next to me for a brief moment. "I'll be seeing you in a couple of weeks when you come to L.A."

He reached out to give me a quick hug.

I stiffened and felt something strong and stony rise up inside myself.

I took a deep breath and cleared my throat. "Howard, I don't think I'll be coming to Los Angeles with you."

Howard looked at me. For a moment he just stared. His bright blue eyes filled with tears before he walked over to the window, fingering the ledge nervously.

Inside a Woman

I stood facing Howard, the half peeled apple in my hand. The room was absolutely still as Howard looked out at the towering evergreens bending under the summer breeze. Then, in a halting voice, he spoke.

"I don't know what's wrong, Jane." He paused to swallow. "But things are going to get better in California. I promise you."

I glanced sideways at the rock garden just outside our Dutch door as the moments passed. Then some wild violets caught my eye, poking up among the stones. They looked as fragile as I suddenly felt inside but watching their brave little heads in the wind prompted a seedling of hope in me.

4
...

To California with a Promise

In the early '60s, southern California attracted thousands of new, young residents who came with great expectations that their lives could be different here.

I bet my entire future on that dream.

When Howard made me that promise in our kitchen in Seattle, I was at the end of my stamina; the pain in my heart, intense and unrelenting.

Even after Howard left for California and I began to arrange for our move from Seattle, a mix of hopes, dreams, and fears accompanied me. What if it didn't work this time? I would have moved again with three young children, set up a home again, connected the wires of our daily lives to a new community, a new routine. Could I do it? Yes. Could Howard and I work out our relationship? That was still the gnawing question.

The children and I flew down to the Burbank Airport on a sunny day in June, 1964. By the time we'd been in Burbank two months, the warm sunny days and relaxed indoor-outdoor living soothed me into believing that I could give it another try.

We moved into a spit-and-polish Cape Code rambler on Tujunga Avenue in Burbank. The street, shaded with trees, ran along the north edge of the city and was one of hundreds of little neighborhoods that stretched throughout the San Fernando Valley, just north of Los Angeles.

During our time there, "beautiful downtown Burbank" began to gain national notoriety from Johnny Carson, host of the popular *Tonight* show that broadcast from NBC Studios, just inside the city limits.

Living in southern California was a new existence for Howard and me. Life in a city bursting with possibility in every direction was heady stuff for two pastors' kids. Suddenly, we found ourselves swimming in a much bigger pond, bigger than we'd ever seen.

By 1965, thousands of young people were lured to Los Angeles and San Francisco with a promise of a new future that they could control. Already, the Beatles had appeared on the Ed Sullivan Show and changed music forever. The Beach Boys' hit, "Wish They All Could Be California Girls," was taken seriously by a new generation charmed by the beckoning arm of a city that promised eternal youth and endless horizons; a place where they could make their own rules.

During those years, British "mod" fashion became a trendy way to dress. Women wore pants called hip-huggers, crop tops, mini-dresses, and white go-go boots. Rock-and-rollers, hippies, and surfers mixed it up together as parks and beaches came alive with spontaneous rock concerts. This was before the underside of drugs was known, and, ignorant of the consequences, Los Angeles quickly became a nonstop party.

I decided right off that if I were going to live in this city, I was going to look like a California girl, too—tanned, streaked blonde hair, with a smile etched in the latest frosty pale lipstick.

Howard's new position as manager of the southwest regional office meant that he commuted over the Hollywood Hills separating "the valley" from Hollywood. The opportunity kept him challenged while I was finding challenges of my own.

The warm weather and casual lifestyle warmed the cocoon of my being enough for me to experience a personal metamorphosis of sorts. At age twenty-nine, I was maturing and growing in confidence. Now I could jump in to be Lisa's Bluebird leader with ease or help with Jeff's Cub Scout troop. Our youngest, Scott, took swimming lessons and we spent days on end at the beach. I felt deeply blessed with these three loving children.

Cooking became a new adventure. Jane, the young bride for whom tuna casserole and meatloaf were an accomplishment, became Jane the hostess who knew her chicken divan from beef bourguignonne. Comfortable with entertaining now, I looked forward to planning dinner parties for a growing circle of friends. Like mixed flowers, these people came in titillating variety.

Even in Burbank, with many of its small-town ways still intact, the impact of Los Angeles brought Howard and me into a new social life with people in the entertainment industry, stock brokers, lawyers, mixed with an occasional colorful character that southern California parties are known for.

Although our idea of play meant that we shared

oceanside picnics and volleyball on Santa Monica Beach instead of love-ins and rock concerts, Howard and I were convinced that these people really knew how to have fun.

Even though Howard and I maintained many of the values we grew up with during our Burbank years, I was not yet open to the Lord's gentle guidance. I didn't know Christ personally yet. Instead, I pursued life on my terms in California, trying to make it fulfilling and meaningful.

I wanted to be happy, and under the warm sun and friendly chatter, I could almost fool myself that I was. But I'd been reared too long in a Christian home to be totally at peace about parts of our new lifestyle.

Howard and I joined a Lutheran church in Glendale, where I encountered an adventure of another kind. I was teaching Vacation Bible School that summer and was drawn into a circle of women who were undeniably filled with joy. This expression was so much different from the kind of surface emotion that passed for happiness among our friends, I needed to know why.

One day, on the way home in the car, I felt comfortable enough with one woman to ask her a simple question: "What's so different about you?"

Her response was direct. "Jane, I have received the baptism in the Holy Spirit."

My obvious interest invited her to continue talking about Jesus, and how His love filled her in a new and powerful way and how she had spoken in tongues, a gift the Holy Spirit had given her. I was intrigued, but wary. I had to admit there was nothing "flaky" about this woman, and I couldn't argue with the reality I saw in her. It was as if something had melted the bedrock of her being and fused into it a peace and joy I couldn't imagine existed.

As I pondered what I saw and what she said, I began to feel a quiet inner sense that surprised me with its normalcy: this experience was not only right, it was also for me.

But when? Or how? I had no idea.

BACK TO THE FUTURE

We had lived in Burbank for almost four years when Howard walked in the front door with a surprise.

"Can you believe it?" he chortled. "We're moving back to Seattle."

It may have surprised me at first, but instinctively, I felt that something good lay ahead. Whether it was my association with these women or the sole working of the Holy Spirit, for the first time in my life, I was actually aware that God was reaching out to me in a personal way.

As our Burbank years had progressed, the never-a-dull-moment days, so exciting at first, became empty rituals of the chicly dressed telling glib jokes over afternoon cocktails. Like a slow leak in a car tire, the lack of substance in our lives in L.A. deflated our early enthusiasm for the laid-back life. Despite our church ties, in those four years, we knew little of a life that sustained us in an affirming, nourishing way.

God moved in my dissatisfaction. The night before the moving van came, my hands went to an old book of my dad's, *The Pursuit of God* by A.W. Tozer. The words on one yellowed page drew me like a parched plant to water:

We pursue God because, and only because, He has first put an urge within us that spurs us to the pursuit. "No man can come to me," said our Lord, "except the Father which hath sent Me draw him." And it is by this very prevenient drawing that God takes us from every vestige of credit for the act of coming. The impulse to pursue God originates with God, but the outworking of that impulse is our following hard after him.[1]

I closed the book and shut my eyes but the words remained illuminated in my mind's eye: We pursue God because he draws us to himself first. Was this really happening? Was God indeed drawing me to Himself?

I, who had not yet known a personal relationship with this God I'd heard of since childhood, fell to my knees beside our bed. Everything in my past and present narrowed to one anguished cry from my heart: God, help me! Please help me to find You and know You personally as You really are.

I did not ask Him into my life that night, but I sensed then that I was finally on the right road in my journey. God was my only hope and moving back to Seattle was an important step in His direction.

TRUDGING ON

Had I known that I would wallow through another year in Seattle, filled with emptiness and frustration, my heart might have failed right then. I still carried guilt around like rocks in a gunny sack. There were times when I wondered if my lack of peace despite my efforts was my punishment for the failure of my first marriage.

Once we got settled in Seattle, I joined a small Bible study that met in women's homes. The group was congenial and the fellowship was warm, but our discussions centered on the intellect rather than the heart.

One morning, rather than keep my pain inside myself, I took a risk. I told them what was going on in my life. But I didn't know how much my hurt would show until my voice began to quaver and tears formed in my eyes.

An awkward silence followed. I dabbed at my eyes with

a handkerchief and took a deep breath.

In a few moments, as if nothing had happened, the discussion picked up right where it paused before I spoke.

We adjourned, and I walked to my car alone. Then the floodgates burst open. I hurt in my marriage, and ten-year-old Jeff was beginning to have some struggles that increased my pain, just as my brother, Jimmy's rebellion in Glendale, tore at my mother and father.

Sitting there in the car with tears falling on my lap, I knew I had to get to God.

THE HEALING WORD

I drove home immediately and sat down at the kitchen table for another cup of coffee. I reached for my Bible and opened it aimlessly to the Book of Lamentations. My eyes fell directly on the third chapter, seventh verse: "He hath hedged me about, that I cannot get out. He hath made my chain heavy" (3:7 KJV).

Incredulous, I read it over several times. It was as if the scripture had my name on it. That's exactly how I felt—wanting to run as far as I could, but totally trapped and hedged in.

There was no other word for what happened to me in the next few moments than "revelation." God spoke to me through His Word, transcending my mind and penetrating my heart. In a few brief minutes, Truth unraveled itself with unbelievable speed and undeniable clarity.

I glanced out the kitchen window at the backyard fence. All that had gone before me, the sin, the sorrow, the pain, the disappointment, was not what God wanted for me. But His love was using it to build fences, fences that hedged me into a relationship with Him. This was not a second-hand relationship interpreted through the minds and hearts of parents or friends, but a relationship for me alone.

I knew positively that I was about to experience God's love firsthand and feel His personal touch on my personal needs. I knew, too, that the key lay in knowing Jesus. Not the Jesus I knew about—the historical figure I thought of in Sunday School stories, but a Jesus I could know. Really know.

I poured myself another cup of coffee and opened to the New Testament. Here I was, a woman unfamiliar with her Bible, stumbling across life-giving passages at my kitchen table. I turned to Matthew and again read words directed at my heart. " 'Your heavenly Father knoweth that ye have need of all these things' " (6:32 KJV).

What a concept! It hit me with laser precision. And it kept expanding as I sat there reading. God was *my* Father. He had used an earthly mother and father to bring me forth, but I was really His. He was the Creator of everything, seen and unseen. He knew me like no one knew me. In His love, He allowed life to teach this "good little girl" who always tried to do everything right, allowing circumstances to prod and shape me to a point of knowing she was a sinner in need of a Savior.

Like the father in the Prodigal Son story of Luke 15, my Heavenly Father was waiting for me. I could relate to every line of that familiar parable Jesus told. The son who squandered his inheritance in the far country finally came to his senses. " 'I will set out and go back to my father' " (v. 18). The story could have been written just for me.

But there's more. I began to feel the impact of the rest of this story: the extraordinary move on the father's part— that embarrassingly emotional move. Seeing his wayward son afar off, the father runs to him to embrace him. (See Luke 15:20).

Loving Father, needy daughter. The Lord Himself and Jane. She was coming home to the Father and He had run out to meet her with His outstretched arms. He knew me inside out as no one else had—or would ever know me.

In that moment, sensing His presence with me in the kitchen, I knew He could instantly speak everything in my life into perfect order—every longing, every hurt, every frustration, every need I had.

I was glued to the passage that went on to say that I needed to seek first the Kingdom of God and His righteousness and all these things would be added to me. (See Matt. 6:33).

Joy Dawson, internationally known Bible teacher, has often said, "God loves desperate prayers." That morning, I closed my Bible and prayed one:

"Lord, if I never spend another happy day in this life, I am going to seek You and Your Kingdom first. And I choose to trust You to add to me what I need."

I had come home at last.

5
...

A New Dimension

Remember that portion of John's gospel where Jesus tells His disciples that He will be leaving them? (See John 13:31–14:16). I can only imagine how that news must have shaken these men. No doubt some were stunned to silence. Others, like Peter, Thomas, and Philip, peppered their Master with questions: "Where are You going?" "Why?" And perhaps the most burning question in their hearts, "What's going to happen to us?"

I love the way Jesus answers his little, ragtag band of followers: Not only would Jesus be leaving, He warned them that the days ahead would be anything but a Sunday School picnic. " 'They will put you out of the synagogue; in fact, a time is coming when anyone who kills you will think he is offering a service to God' " (John 16:2).

This wasn't your typical retirement party with gold watches and glorious predictions for the future; this talk was of separation, hardship, and death. Jesus knew full well that they wouldn't comprehend it all.

But they were staggered by the impact of these words. Did these grief-stricken men miss the nugget of good news Jesus neatly dropped on them? " 'But I tell you the truth: It is for your good that I am going away. Unless I go away, the Counselor (the Holy Spirit) will not come to you' " (John 16:7).

How could it be?

It would be days before they had any answers, days filled with loneliness, fear, and excruciating sorrow over the death of their Lord. Demoralized, they couldn't even recall—let alone believe—Jesus' promise of hope: " 'You will grieve, but your grief will turn to joy' " (John 16:20).

They hadn't counted on a miracle-working God, one who grasped his Son from the grip of death, foiling Satan's plans. Jesus, the world's Redeemer, was alive and well! His words were true; He was with the Father. Then, as promised, like the sound of a mighty, rushing wind, He dispatched the Holy Spirit from heaven to fill the disciples' hearts at the Jewish festival of Pentecost in Jerusalem (Acts 2:1-40).

The disciples began preaching boldly in the streets of Jerusalem, boldly declaring that the resurrected Jesus was both Lord and Christ.

Courage! Empowerment! Joy so uninhibited it provoked onlookers to say, "They have had too much wine" (Acts 2:13). But they were not drunk. They were filled to overflowing with the Holy Spirit promised by their Savior, Jesus Christ.

Larry Christianson, Lutheran renewal leader, echoes this same fact. "From the day of Pentecost onward, the coming of the Spirit has been inseparably linked with telling people what God has done, is doing, and will do through Christ and the giving of His Holy Spirit.[1]

"'It is for your good that I am going away'" (John 16:7). For our good? Yes!

Jesus' words are clear and He's never taken them back. The empowering of the Holy Spirit was normal for believers in the early church. The Spirit continues to be poured out so that Christ's followers—His church—can carry the message of hope and salvation into the world.

At the turn of the twentieth century, the Lord poured out his Holy Spirit in a dramatic way in California in what came to be known as the Azusa Street Revival.

Supernatural gifts of the Spirit were manifested everywhere—healings, tongues, prophecies. Many said it was the "work of the enemy," and that it would soon "blow over."

They were right. It blew all over the world.[2]

By 1960, the winds of the Holy Spirit were blowing in mainline churches. By 1967, the winds began to blow in the Roman Catholic church. By 1977, nearly all the denominations had been touched.

From small beginnings in the early 1900s to the present day, an estimated 411 million people around the world have been baptized in the Holy Spirit.

No wonder Jesus said that his leaving would be a good thing.

A PERSONAL FILLING

I didn't know about the solid history of the Holy Spirit's work when I first listened to my Lutheran friend's story about her baptism in the Holy Spirit that day in Burbank.

I knew, since that Seattle morning in my kitchen, that I was the Lord's child, that I now had a personal relationship with Jesus Christ. I also knew I had a lot to learn.

Now, back in Seattle, I discovered my sister-in-law, Elaine, also had this experience with the Holy Spirit. She was a solid, mainline church member, and a woman I well respected. I was still uncertain, yet I couldn't deny the change in her.

Others were talking about the power of the Holy Spirit for our day and about what was happening in mainline churches during the late '60s and early '70s.

Two books fell into my hands, *They Speak with Other Tongues* by John and Elizabeth Sherrill and *Nine O'Clock in the Morning* by Dennis Bennett, rector of St. Luke's Episcopal Church in Seattle.

I devoured both books and things began adding up for me. My fears were being dissipated under the gentle drawing I first felt that day in Burbank after my friend shared her experience. It was an appointment I needed to keep.

I knew I had to get myself to the Friday night meeting at St. Luke's where Dennis Bennett talked about the baptism in the Holy Spirit. One evening, I drove with a friend to the Ballard district, and walked in.

Seated in the back of the church, I listened as Father Bennett talked about how the Holy Spirit was poured out at Pentecost. He not only described the events Luke records in the book of *Acts*, but he shared his own experience of being filled with the Holy Spirit and receiving the gift of tongues.

Next, a man named Stanley gave a "message in tongues." I'd never heard anything like it before. It was beautiful, rhythmical, like someone speaking in another language.

Silence followed until a gray-haired lady named Edna stepped forward, faced the audience, and gave the interpretation in English, speaking in the exact rhythmic pattern Stanley spoke in.

I knew in the deepest part of my being that *this was the*

Holy Spirit. My reservations about this truth dissolved.

I could not leave that meeting without going forward to be prayed for to receive the baptism in the Holy Spirit. My mouth was dry, my knees shook, but I made my way to the altar and asked the Holy Spirit to fill me.

I waited, as the others at the altar quietly began speaking in a heavenly language, but I had no such manifestation at the time. I walked away thinking, this didn't happen to me . . . maybe it won't happen to me.

For several weeks, I struggled intellectually with my feelings about the gifts of the Spirit. Is this all for real? Are they for our day?

Some weeks later, in a phone conversation, a longtime friend strongly encouraged me. "Jane, you need to make a decision. Do you really believe this is true or not?"

My quick answer surprised me. "I believe it!" I hung up the phone and went directly into my bedroom and began praying. Miraculously, a heavenly language came pouring from my lips. The heavens opened as I'd never experienced, bathing me in waves of the Father's love. I was vitally aware of the presence of Jesus in a new way.

My heart flooded over with the deep realization of being accepted, loved, and forgiven. I didn't want to leave the room, but when I eventually stood to my feet, I remember saying to myself, "This is real."

WALKING IN A NEW DIMENSION

After my baptism in the Holy Spirit, I began to discover Christ's "good thing" dimension in my life.

This Jesus who I heard about all my life was no longer shrouded in the pages of my childhood Sunday School papers or hidden in the verses of an old gospel hymn.

He was real. Alive. A Friend. A Companion. A Loving Presence. Never in my life had I experienced anything like this—actually feeling Jesus' love and loving him in return.

From the first moment I experienced the release of a heavenly prayer language, it was as if someone turned on the light switch.

Prayer became easy and natural, like having an intimate conversation with a best friend. I had a hunger for God's Word in a way I had never experienced. The Word of God opened to me. Scriptures I'd previously read came alive. Another extraordinary difference came, unannounced, through the back door of my heart: For the first time in my life, I sensed the thirst in my soul and the ache in my heart diminish.

How do you share such a tremendous spiritual experience?

Before I had time even to think about how I might tell Howard and the others around me, the Lord impressed me to be quiet for a time about what had happened.

SHARING MY STORY

One evening, a year later, Howard and I were talking in our kitchen as we finished dinner. I pushed back my chair and moved to the counter to cut our pie for dessert.

I filled our coffee cups, and eased back into my chair. "Howie," I began, "I want to tell you something that happened to me awhile back . . . something really significant."

Howard put his fork down and looked expectantly across the table. Simply and directly, I told him about my experience with the Holy Spirit.

For a full minute, Howard said nothing. I waited for his response, feeling curious, and at peace. When it came, it was tender and affirming, again, strong evidence of the way the Holy Spirit comes alongside as a "helper."

"I don't understand it at all, Jane, but I'll tell you one thing." Howard paused. "I can't deny the truth of it because of the change I see in you."

THE WORD OF THE HOUR

Change was the word of the hour. What happened to me in 1969 was happening to thousands of others experiencing the baptism in the Holy Spirit. Praise meetings, teaching tapes, and Bible studies swept across the U.S. It was a season where faith was high and prayers seemed to be answered quickly, as believers discovered the reality of a supernatural God.

By 1970, I was headed in a new direction. My schedule, priorities, my concerns all began to focus on a life where God was a living reality. I was energized by my new relationship with Jesus and by studying and teaching the Bethel Bible Study Series at church. Still, I hungered to know even more about the practical outworking of the Spirit-filled life.

In September of 1971, I invited Shade O'Driscoll, the co-rector's wife of St. Luke's Episcopal Church, to our home on a Thursday morning to share her testimony and bring her teaching on womanhood. Eight women came. Soon others were asking if they could also attend. The group grew. And grew.

"How many did you have today?" Invariably, Howard asked me for a count every Thursday night when he came home for dinner. We had agreed to open our home for whomever God would bring. But in our wildest imaginations, neither of us had any idea that this group would explode. Thirty-five to forty women came on a regular basis for two years.

Many days, sixty women would squeeze in. Occasionally, eighty, and once, a hundred women took up every inch of our living room. They came by word-of-mouth: friends, neighbors, friends of friends. Many Thursday mornings, I'd open the door and find complete strangers on my porch. And they all asked the same question. "Is this the house where someone is teaching a Bible study?"

Women drove across town to hear about the Holy Spirit and receive His gifts. Like hungry children, we were learning together how to walk in a new dimension.

MY AGLOW BEGINNINGS

One afternoon in 1972, a friend, Paula Shields, invited me to a home prayer meeting. Her invitation seemed a bit vague.

"What's this all about?" I quizzed her. "Does this group meet on a regular basis?" I was curious that, with my current associations with Christian women, I hadn't heard of a group called Aglow.

Paula was enthusiastic, but noncommittal, and I was interested enough to join her.

At the meeting, the prayer emphasis centered on finding new leadership for the Edmonds Aglow gathering. I sat quietly enjoying my coffee and the fellowship as the women counted the secret ballots and one announced, "Joanie Johnson will be vice-president and, Jane, you'll be the new Edmonds Aglow president."

I nearly dropped my coffee in my lap. "Me? You've got to be kidding!"

The very thought of standing in front of people made my stomach queasy. It wasn't that I didn't want to be available to the Lord, it was that this would involve me in areas for which I knew I had no natural giftings. I simply couldn't do it.

"I have trouble praying in front of others," I stammered. "I'm the one who quit speech class in high school."

My protestations, however, didn't deter these women. Sensing my shock and apprehension, immediately they gathered around me, laid hands on me, and prayed. One by one, they promised their support. While they insisted they'd been led by the Holy Spirit to choose me, I jokingly told them later that it felt more like "holy arm twisting!"

Knowing I was unfamiliar with Aglow, Paula shared the history and vision of the group with me. It began in 1967, when four Seattle women met to seek the Lord about forming a group that would provide interdenominational Christian fellowship for women. By 1972, it had incorporated with sixty fellowships established across the United States. Neither Paula nor I knew at the time that God would provide stunning growth for Aglow in those next years: Aglow boards would be established in Canada, Israel, Australia, Lebanon, India, the Netherlands, Mexico, New Zealand, Nigeria, Kenya and Ghana.

Surprisingly, it was born in north Seattle, not far from where I now lived. Soon after, another group formed in Edmonds, a small town just north of Seattle. Drawing twenty-five to thirty women to a restaurant every month, the group gave women a chance to worship the Lord and share testimonies of what God was doing by His Spirit.

WHAT NOW?

As the new president of Edmonds Aglow, I considered the immediate future.

Joanie Johnson and I met together the next day but all we could do was stare at each other and ask, "What shall we do?" We hadn't the faintest idea of where to start.

So we prayed.

We agreed to start by finding a meeting place. We wanted an attractive room where women would feel comfortable coming for lunch and inviting friends to join

Inside a Woman

them. We scoured the area, but kept coming back to a beautiful spot on the waterfront, the Edmonds Yacht Club. I was positive this was the place. The lower level faced the water, a lovely room overlooking Puget Sound and the Olympic Mountains. We met the manager and he was interested in having us. There would be no charge for the room, but there was a catch: We had to guarantee that at least one hundred women would come.

Joanie and I stood in the room with the manager that day, looking out at the lofty mountains and the afternoon sun casting its shadow across the choppy Puget Sound water. Rows of expensive sail boats moored in front of us, bobbed back and forth in the waves—an incongruous picture against our non-existent treasury.

Faith often feels foolish. And it did that day.

We had no money, but I turned to the manager and said, "We promise you one hundred women."

The new board met in my home. Our first "board meeting" became a time of praying and worshipping.

Leave it to women! And to the Lord. When we prayed, the heavens seemed to open in response to our praises. When it came time for business, ideas flowed in unanimity. That day we decided to invite a speaker, decorate with fresh flowers, have a centerpiece on the head table, use white linens, and serve a buffet luncheon attractively on silver trays.

Despite the strong support from the board, Joanie and I exchanged more than one anxious moment over the phone prior to that first meeting at the yacht club. Would anyone come? The worrying turned out to be a waste of time.

More than one hundred women came that day.

For the next two years, the Edmonds group had a flourishing life of its own. It was rare that they had less than 125 women; sometimes as many as 350 women came to worship and fellowship in the power of the Holy Spirit and hear a variety of speakers share the Word of the Lord.

A SEASON OF SERVANTHOOD

During the time I was president of the Edmonds group in 1972, I also agreed to fill out the term of the recording secretary at the recently established Aglow headquarters office in Edmonds.

Just after I finished the recording secretary's term, I was asked to be the vice-president for the Washington State Aglow. I accepted that position and served for a year.

However, when the selection committee met to determine the officers for the following year and asked me to continue, I was reluctant. In fact, I sensed the Lord was saying that this was not a door I was to walk through. I felt him say, "Come away, my beloved; spend time with me."

A tug of war ensued, mostly inside me. The selection committee was persistent.

"Jane, we have prayed and fasted and everyone on our committee still comes up with your name. Won't you reconsider?"

Their reasoning was persuasive; I did not want to miss the Lord's true leading. At the same time, I couldn't dismiss the inner "No" I kept hearing.

Torn and afraid I'd misunderstood the voice inside me, I called my dad for counsel. My parents had recently retired to Edmonds and our family, greatly healed from our past, was enjoying a new closeness.

"Am I hearing right, Dad? All the women on the committee insist that the Lord has given them my name."

Dad's voice was warm and assuring. "Honey, God wants you to hear His voice above all others. Trust what you hear God saying to you." And I did.

A SERVANT'S HEART

I was excused from Aglow leadership, and back home in my comfort zone I had no obligations except for my family. The kids were busy in school, Howard was traveling some, and I had days to myself to read, pray, and do the creative things that always gave me such pleasure: baking, gardening, a little redecorating.

One day, I phoned a friend who'd attended the prayer meetings in my home. Frances was a lovely women, confined to a wheelchair with multiple sclerosis. She mentioned that she needed someone to help her three days a week, but she wanted the woman to be a Christian.

Frances hadn't finished talking when I felt clearly impressed with the words, "You're the one, Jane." Part of the urge was financial: I'd been looking anxiously at an account I needed to pay off and this seemed like an opportunity. But much more than that, I sensed it was the Lord's leading.

Frances lived in a beautiful Tudor home, tucked back among a grove of evergreen trees above Puget Sound. I was with her three days a week for a year and a half. Totally responsible for all her personal care, I also fixed lunch, started dinner, and did the laundry as well as light housekeeping.

None of it was drudgery.

A few months prior to this job, I'd heard a speaker share on servanthood at an Aglow area retreat. I remember leaving that meeting pondering, I wonder what it really means to be a servant.

One day, as I was drying Frances' feet after her morning bath, an answer came in that tender, quiet voice of the Holy Spirit, "I am teaching you to have the heart of a servant."

HOW COULD THEY UNDERSTAND?

Like so many of life's valuable experiences, my working for Frances wasn't totally understood by those around me. Howard kiddingly called me his "little domestic." Friends were sincerely puzzled about "Jane's job," and were determined to get a satisfactory explanation from me. "I can't believe you're doing this," was the usual opening gambit. "Since when did you decide to become a maid?" I had no answers for their ears. How could I communicate the inexplicable joy of ministering to my friend? Telling them I was "on assignment" from the Lord sounded almost foolish, coming from a woman with a comfortable house in the suburbs and a husband with a good job.

Alone much of the time, Frances was spiritually hungry and eagerly awaited my arrival each morning. Amazingly, I was just as eager to come. It was as if our hearts were being knit together as we interacted during the daily schedule that made up her routine.

I started each day by giving her exercises for her legs and feet. We followed with her bath. After I dressed her, the highlight of the day was our fellowship, sharing the Lord, and praying together. Those shared moments were what God spontaneously produced between us throughout the day.

Something else was happening inside me. It was as if I were being fitted for an internal wardrobe change. At first, I'd felt as if I were walking around, bundled up in a heavy wool coat, clutching my scarf to my neck, but gradually the heavy clothes were taken off until one day, I suddenly realized that I was dashing about, light as a ballerina in a chiffon dress.

The more I poured myself out to serve Frances, the less I cared what other people thought of me. The facade of acceptability that I'd built around myself and my family began to disintegrate. This was not the stuff of great spiritual revelation. It was simply something I was walking through, an interlude in my life in which God was teaching me abundant lessons in humility as well as deeply satisfying me with the joy of serving.

My year and a half with Frances flew by. On my last day with her, we said our tearful goodbyes. As I walked to my car, a verse from John's gospel whispered to my heart: "'I no longer call you [servant]. . . . Instead, I have called you [friend]'" (John 15:15).

I started the car and looked back at the brilliant purple heather blooming along the driveway of Frances' lovely home. All I could say as I pulled out was, "Thank you, Lord."

A NEW FAMILY CRISIS

My life was full of a growing awareness of the Holy Spirit and His power and in my new-found joy in walking with others who, like I was, were learning to walk in the Spirit.

But it was not perfect. There were still problems in our home. In fact, one of them was escalating.

None of us realized at the time, how traumatic our move from California in 1969 had been for my son, Jeff. Like my brother, Jimmy, who left his friends and relationships back in Akron, Jeff left behind friends he had grown close to during our four years in California. Finding his niche with the kids in his new school in Edmonds proved difficult for a sixth grader heading into puberty with all its physical and emotional upheaval.

Jeff's sixth grade teacher noted that he was struggling. "Jeff's a tender-hearted boy. With his sensitivity, I can see how he easily feels frustrated and defeated. Then, to compensate, he becomes the class clown. It's typical of kids his age to want his peers' acceptance."

Unfortunately, Jeff's search for approval eventually led to his "hanging around" with kids who were also struggling with feeling good about themselves—and who were experimenting with smoking and dressing in counter-cultural style.

Jeff began bringing home poor report cards, or skipping school altogether. Associating with at-loose-ends kids, his behavior alarmed us all. But it was especially tough on Howard. Jeff and Howard were colliding at almost every turn.

During those years, Howard reacted strongly. He instinctively did what he knew to do from his own father: he tightened the rules.

The stricter Howard became, the more Jeff resisted. Jeff continued to drift closer to his "tough guy" friends.

By high school, Jeff was in full-blown rebellion. Hair down to his shoulders, headbands, ratty jackets, and torn jeans were his rebellious labels. He looked and acted like the prototype hard rocker of the '70s.

As Jeff's mother, I was beside myself with worry. I was caught in the middle between Jeff and Howard, believing Howard's approach to discipline was too severe.

At the same time, I felt Howard didn't realize the extent of the situation. I was sure that Jeff was on drugs. "There's more to this than the ordinary teenage rebellion." I pleaded with Howard to consider the possibility.

"He'll be all right, Jane," Howard countered. "He just needs some good, old-fashioned discipline." Like so many fathers, Howard couldn't bring himself to see such a problem in his own son. His solution was denial, anger, and more rules.

Nothing anyone did stemmed the tide of Jeff's downward spiral. By his junior year in high school, he dropped out of school altogether. Now, clearly on marijuana, other drugs, and alcohol, he was in and out of the house, out sometimes for days at a time—whereabouts unknown.

In the meantime, the rest of us were being torn apart by the confusion and tension that this kind of behavior breeds. Anyway you looked at it, we were living a nightmare. I was sick with worry, Howard manifested his worry in anger, and Lisa and Scott were scared to death.

A NIGHT TO REMEMBER

One event stands out as a dreadful reminder of the toll Jeff's actions were taking on our family.

In July of 1975, Howard and I, along with Lisa and Scott, took a ten-day trip in a motor home with family friends from California. Together, we headed up to Banff and Lake Louise to vacation in the beautiful Canadian Rockies. Because Jeff was working, we felt comfortable leaving him at home.

Making good time on our return trip, we arrived back home several hours earlier than we expected. I walked up to the front porch, put my key in the lock, opened the door, and stepped into a darkened house with all the drapes pulled.

That undeniable sickly sweet smell hit me full force in the face. Marijuana. I wanted to scream out every ounce of breath I'd taken in. With one hand I covered my mouth and with the other, I groped for the light switch. I needed a steadying hand. "Howard, please come quick!"

Alarmed at my tone, Howard ran past our friends and stopped next to me in the entrance hall. Lisa and Scott squeezed by us, their mouths falling open at the disaster before them in the living room. "Look at your chair, Mom." Scott ran to lift the overstuffed chair that was on its side by an overturned lamp.

Howard, now in action, carefully checked out the rest of the house. I stood still in the entrance hall, unable to move further.

By now, Scott had reported the beer bottles and cigarette burns on the coffee table. Lisa yelled from downstairs, "I can't even open the laundry room door. It's piled too high with people's dirty clothes."

Howard stalked back to my side, his body trembling with anger, "Jane, somebody threw up on our bed."

My stomach turned and my knees went weak. I swirled around to Howard and buried my head in his chest. I couldn't believe Jeff would allow this to happen. "Oh, Howie, we've been through so much with this kid." I was utterly undone.

A CRY FOR HELP

Hours later, after the house had been aired, vacuumed, and scrubbed, and I dropped into bed, a light knock sounded at our bedroom door.

It was Lisa, standing in her nightgown. Her blue eyes wide open, she looked at my face with great sadness. I pulled her over to sit closely on my side of the bed and started gently rubbing her back. "Pretty tough homecoming, Lisa."

Tears trickled down her cheeks. She turned her head toward me and her eyes briefly searched mine for answers. "Mom, how could Jeff do this to us?"

Reaching for lotion on the bed stand, I continued to stroke her back and neck. "He needs help, Lisa. In fact, we all do."

She was silent for a minute, allowing me to stroke away some of the hurt she felt. Then I felt her back muscles tense again as she added poignantly, "And you know, Mom, he didn't even help us clean up."

I told Lisa the truth, Jeff's behavior was a cry for help. Yet I was at my wit's end about what to do.

Howard and I couldn't talk openly about it; we couldn't seem to connect at the heart level, let alone pray together over the problem. It was obvious that we had a grave situation on our hands. Everyone in the family was hurting and I was the hand-wringing mother, terrified of the effects of Jeff's wrong choices. I saw him as a confused teenager, smoking, drinking, and drugging his days away, falling prey to the attacks of Satan.

Was I going to lose my son?

A NEW DIMENSION IN PRAYER

One afternoon, I left the Aglow office and walked to my car, got in, and drove home, not unlike a robot. Words are inadequate to describe the sorrow that rose up in me. This was a wrenching heartbrokenness deep within.

No one was home when I pulled in. I walked directly upstairs to our bedroom, went into our walk-in closet, and closed the door. I felt I had to be alone in a place where I could physically groan.

Unsure of what was happening in me, I calmly took authority over any activity of Satan. Then I said, "Lord, I yield to you." I waited . . . and waited.

From the pit of my insides, a weeping welled up in me that was unlike any weeping I'd ever experienced. It burst forth in deep, inarticulate groans, giving expression to the agony within me.

I wailed over my family, "Oh, God, establish Your Kingdom in our home."

Those were the only words I spoke and I repeated them over and over, the burden of my soul coming forth with more groaning and travail.

I don't know how long I was in my closet that day. All I

know was that I felt like a woman in her first labor. She doesn't know what to expect, but her time has come and there is no turning back. I had no alternative but to give myself to this work—for days and weeks to come.

Most days, my praying began with this same deep weeping. I cried out my petitions to God, speaking out loud for all of my family: "Oh God, establish Your throne in Howard's heart. Protect Lisa and Scott from any ungodly influence. Turn Jeff's heart back to You."

I spoke Scripture out into the atmosphere. I declared to the enemy that he had gone this far and he could go no further in the Hansen household. To mark that declaration, I went from my front door to every door post in the house and spoke out strongly in the name of Jesus: "I push back the forces of darkness and I call forth light."

My confidence grew as I yielded up every member of my family to God and declared His promises over them. And where Jeff was concerned, I prayed, "Lord, I release him to You. I don't just want a young man who is cleaned up and off drugs. Do whatever You have to do to bring forth a man of God."

One day during this time, a scripture passage that I'd heard Jack Hayford, internationally known teacher, speak on came to me like a special delivery set of instructions: "Sing, O barren woman, you who never bore a child; burst into song, shout for joy, you who were never in labor; because more are the children of the desolate woman than of her who has a husband" (Isa. 54:1).

After that day, I began to sing to the spiritually barren areas in our family and invite the Holy Spirit to have authority over our home. "Enlarge the place of your tent, stretch your tent curtains wide. . . . Do not fear disgrace; you will not be humiliated" (Isa. 54:2, 4).

I spoke God's promises out loud as I worked around the

house, dismantling the "barrenness," by faith and calling forth fruitfulness.

Of course, I was a woman of prayer, but before this time, I never considered myself an intercessor. I always thought that intercessors were "a select few" who closeted themselves away on big assignments from God.

In retrospect, I can see that I didn't just wake up one day and decide to pray for my family. Without a doubt, a "spirit of intercession" had come upon me. God, by His Holy Spirit, did something outside myself.

Would I ever know the results of this prayer?

Yes, that day would come. At the time, however, obedience was the issue. Still, in the next few months, I witnessed many hopeful signs that fruit was growing within our family.

HOWARD'S HEART

Over the last few years, I could see the Holy Spirit drawing Howard to Jesus. Through a couples' fellowship in our home, a dramatic deliverance from a long-entrenched smoking habit, a miraculous healing of phlebitis while hospitalized, God, in His creative timing, wooed Howard to Himself.

While on a business trip to Montana, he read a book by Don Basham, popular teacher and writer (now deceased). The words touched him in a deep and personal way. Alone in a hotel room, he called out to God and surrendered his life to Him, saying, "I want whatever You have for me."

Even though as a young boy, he had a meaningful and spiritual experience when he was confirmed in the Lutheran Church, he chose not to live in the light of that experience.

That night in Montana was Howard's point of conversion.

Two days later, while he was driving to Cody, Wyoming,

he began to pray aloud, asking Jesus to baptize him with the Holy Spirit. To his utter amazement a new language began to come forth. He knew it was the beginning of a new walk with the Lord.

He called me immediately to share the "good news." When I picked up the phone, I heard excitement in Howard's voice. "Jane, guess what happened to me this afternoon? You won't believe it!" From Cody, Wyoming, my husband's jubilant voice continued.

But I did believe it. Right in the middle of cowboy country, the Holy Spirit was rounding up Howard. We were headed into a new dimension in our family.

Howard's taste of the Spirit's presence in such a profound way gave me a new sense of thanksgiving. I remembered my own experience of the loving presence of Jesus drawing me to Himself, filling me with no less than His supernatural life.

But there was more.

God was at work to bring healing and wholeness to Howard and me and to our entire family. God, in His immense love, wanted to teach me about obedience and servanthood first. Now I was learning to be His warrior/intercessor over my home and loved ones. Only after those lessons had been learned, would I be able to understand the next one.

I was about to enter one of the greatest instruction periods of my life as I became a student/patient with the Master Teacher.

This instruction period would require me to submit my heart, despite more pain, to the Master Surgeon for radical surgery. Finally, I was ready.

6
...

Going for the Heart

The Bible is filled with stories of people with flawed hearts. People who made mistakes, who told lies, who didn't raise their children well. Think about these Old Testament examples: a patriarch whose cowardice caused his wife to be given for a king's pleasure; a brother who deceived his father to gain his blessing; a man groomed to be the leader of the Israelite nation, whose hot temper led him to kill an Egyptian; a king who committed adultery and tried to cover it with murder.

The New Testament stories are just as graphic: a disciple whose bravado gives way to betrayal; followers of Jesus who squabble over being first; a woman caught in adultery; another oppressed with demon spirits. As Bible teacher, Dr. Herbert Lockyer has said, "Sinners by birth become more or less sinners by practice."[1]

Spiritually flawed hearts are only repaired by the Master Surgeon just as physical hearts demand attention from an experienced cardiologist.

An early Seattle pioneer in pediatric and adult heart surgery, and an outspoken man of faith, Dr. Lester Sauvage, recently gave a newspaper interview shortly after his retirement. "The human heart beats 40 million times a year. By the time you're twenty-five years old, it has beat about one billion times, working in a tireless manner to propel nourishment through 60,000 miles of blood vessels . . . nourishment to every one of the 60 trillion cells in the body."[2]

This man, who has seen 4,000 to 5,000 human hearts, who has studied and repaired them, still speaks of them with awe. "You know when you look at things like this that there has to be a God."[3]

Belgian cardiologist, Dr. Noubar Boyadjian, notes in his book, *The Heart*: "Since the beginning of time, the heart has been the symbol of the most precious thing the human race possesses: love . . . the most intimate central point of the human person."[4]

Love. The heart. Even flawed hearts.

When human beings shy away from those of us whose hearts are in pain, Jesus comes to us in our need, confident in His ability to bring forth health and thus allow our hearts to function as they were intended.

Jesus offered His understanding heart to notorious sinners who approached Him. He allowed women to touch Him with their gifts of adoration, without a word of condemnation. He looked at their hearts. His mission was to forgive, and to heal hearts broken in shame and hardened by wrong choices. By the power of His shed blood, He is still doing that today.

I know, because that's what He did for me.

THE SYMPTOMS SURFACE

How does a good little girl like me end up needing heart surgery? Just as years of cholesterol build-up, wrong dietary habits, smoking, and stress eventually damage the physical heart, my years of undealt with hurt in my heart gradually turned to anger as surely as cholesterol blocks arteries.

None of this happens overnight. It's progressive. Insidiously so. My hurt would go underground for long periods of time. Then, a situation, a remark, a disappointment would act like a bellows over a dying fire, infusing it with enough oxygen to burn all day. That's what mine did; it burst into flames of anger.

If you'd seen me in my home, you might have wanted to protest this description because I could function so well. The atmosphere in our home was congenial. Howard and I entertained friends, kept busy with the kids, and life went on.

But underneath the surface, I had become a boiling pot filled with anger. Hurt from my marriage merged with the hurt from my childhood that was never dealt with, that never stopped telling me, "There's no time for you; you're unlovable." Undealt with hurt becomes anger.

Undealt with anger becomes bitterness.

FLASHPOINT

One Saturday morning as Howard and I finished repotting our deck baskets, I opened up with my same old battery of questions. "Why can't I seem to connect with you, Howie?"

The pain of my loneliness prodded me on that morning and I pushed the old issue out again. "Why do you keep distancing yourself from me?"

99

Inside a Woman

Head down, holding a hose to flush off the walk under the deck, Howard ignored my questions and instead of an answer, he said, "If we don't get this moss off the concrete, we'll have to get someone in here with a jack hammer and break this stuff up."

"Jack hammer!" His words hit me like a slap and I stormed into the house, kicked off my yard shoes, and flung my garden gloves across the kitchen table. Easy enough for you to understand how to break up cement, I thought, but I can't seem to pound anything into your head about us, no matter how hard I try. Howard followed me into the kitchen, and our raised voices reverberated throughout the house.

Little explosions like these always calmed down after awhile, but more and more my anger was creeping out at the edges. I couldn't keep it in any longer.

Too many years of trying to please, trying not to rock the boat had gone by. The obedient child. The nice wife. I'd had too many years of feeling as if no one cared or even heard.

Resentment filled me to overflowing. Just like the person needing heart surgery, the day comes when you need help so badly, you don't care how much it hurts because nothing can hurt worse than what you're experiencing.

That's where I was.

Everything was out of control in our home. Jeff, an alcoholic and drug addict, two other hurting children, and a marriage that was sifting like sand through my fingers meant we were on our way to an emotional emergency ward. Howard and I had to get help.

One day, I stood in front of the bathroom mirror and said, "I can't deal with this pain and anger any longer. Someone has got to listen to me."

NO TURNING BACK

Doctors have told me that heart surgery has its moment of truth.

It comes just after the blue-gowned, white-masked surgical team moves into place around the patient.

Silence. Then the raised scalpel, the quick incision. It is not a pretty sight; blood gushes forth and clamps move in to stem the flow.

The surgeon has made his commitment and he does not turn back, despite his knowledge that the patient is undergoing trauma and the recovery will be painful.

In the same way, the Holy Spirit stands ready to repair our spiritual hearts. I, who had never experienced physical heart problems, was ready to fling myself on God's surgical table and allow him to use his sharpest scalpel: truth . . . deep, healing truth.

APPOINTMENT WITH TRUTH

Several friends of mine had sought help from a pastor and his wife about my age who had a wonderful counseling ministry in a rural church north of us. On their strong recommendation, I phoned Dick and Marilyn Williamson for an appointment.

"Dick," I blurted out, "I feel like a boiling pot, filled with anger and rage. I can't keep the lid on any longer, and it all seems focused on my husband."

We set an appointment date, and I hung up the phone.

Scripture is quick to acknowledge anger as a human emotion and equally quick to warn of its potential danger if left undealt with. Paul's words to the believers at Ephesus are a case in point: "When angry, do not sin; do not ever let your wrath—your exasperation, your fury or indignation—last until the sun goes down. Leave no [such] room or foothold for the devil—give no opportunity to him" (Eph. 4:26, 27 TAB).

According to Dr. Larry Crabb, Christian psychologist and author, "Anger tells us something about ourselves that deserves attention, something that will need to be exposed and changed before we can move along the path to mature love."[5]

In the story of Cain and Abel, we see the classic illustration of runaway, unrepentant anger, with its tragic consequences. Angry that the Lord accepted Abel's offering and rejected his, Cain's reaction was written all over his face. "Then the Lord said to Cain, 'Why are you angry? Why is your face downcast? If you do what is right, will you not be accepted?'" (Gen. 4:6, 7).

At that point, Cain had the perfect opportunity to deal with his anger. He could have approached the Lord and his brother in humility and conquered his raging feelings as well as gained their acceptance.

God even spelled out the danger of retaining anger. "'But if you do not do what is right, sin is crouching at your door; it desires to have you, but you must master it'" (Gen. 4:7).

Closed to repentance and reconciliation, Cain let his anger rule him. His rampaging emotions carried him swiftly into a violent act of revenge: "Now Cain said to his brother Abel, 'Let's go out to the field.' And while they were in the field, Cain attacked his brother Abel and killed him" (Gen. 4:8).

From anger, to hatred, to murder.

Does it seem like a gargantuan leap?

The First Epistle of John clearly reinforces this progression of undealt with anger, again using Cain's life as an example. "Anyone who hates his brother is a murderer, and you know that no murderer has eternal life in him" (I John 3:15).

No doubt about it, when confronted with Scripture, I could no longer hide my anger nor dismiss it as just another natural emotion. I was, in fact, a perfect example: A woman whose anger was spiraling downward to hatred.

SURGERY BEGINS

This is exactly the condition I was in when Howard and I arrived at the Williamson's house. Dick and Marilyn met us as we stood at their doorstep.

Although Howard and I were both smiling on the outside, I was boiling inside. Undoubtedly Dick and Marilyn could see beyond my pretense, but their warm, opening words accepted me without qualification: "How can we help you two?"

We sat together around their table. I started to speak, "Well, we really have problems. . . ." My lip quivered. I sighed deeply into the expectant stillness. Then, I could no longer hold the feelings back. A torrent of tears broke lose.

"Let it go, Jane," Marilyn encouraged as she extended a box of tissues to me. I did. I grabbed a tissue and went ahead, pouring out my frustrations in our marriage, barely stopping for breath as my words tumbled over each other.

All during the time I was speaking, Howard rocked back and forth, nervously trying to look as if he didn't have a care in the world.

Looking back now, it must have been obvious to the Williamsons that we were both in extreme pain, covering and protecting ourselves with different strategies. Until recently, I'd hidden my pain and anger beneath a can-do exterior. Howard joked and laughed to avoid exposing the pain he carried.

By now, I, who hadn't yet confronted my childhood, decided that I had been the one who had worked so hard at making our marriage work. Our problem was clearly one-sided: Howard needed to change.

WHY ME?

In the sessions that followed, Dick Williamson directed most of his comments to me because I was the one who seemed most eager for answers.

Once, Dick looked at me and made an observation that hit me as obvious. "Jane, you're looking to Howard to get your needs met."

I could feel the defensiveness rise up in me.

"Of course I'm expecting Howard to meet my needs," I snapped. "That's why I'm so angry. After all, what is marriage all about, anyway?"

His questioning confused me. I just wanted to move on, to get to the "real counseling," the part where Dick could realize, and authoritatively point out that Howard was responsible for our problems.

But Dick kept addressing me.

Why isn't he talking to Howard? I thought as I sat there.

I came away from those first sessions puzzled and irritated. Why was Howard always getting off the hook? I questioned. Why are the sessions so focused on me, my expectations, my judgments, my anger?

I thought I'd made my case pretty clear. I couldn't understand how Dick and Marilyn, so experienced in counseling, could miss seeing our situation and not tell Howard what to do so that our marriage could be turned around.

Finally at one session, I remember feeling pleased when Dick challenged Howard on his tendency to diffuse serious moments with laughter and jokes.

"Is everything funny to you, Howard?"

Howard was silent as Dick settled back in his chair for what seemed like several long moments of silence. Only the steady ticking of the clock invaded the heavy moment. Then, Dick shifted forward again, laid his arms on the table and leaned toward Howard as he asked quietly, "Howard, tell me about your relationship with Jesus."

Howard cleared his throat. Then he smiled at Dick, trying to look comfortable with the notion that he'd been tossed a question he could answer. "My dad was a pastor," he began, "I've been baptized and confirmed." He added, "We were always in church."

But Dick wasn't satisfied.

"I hear, you, Howard. But I'm asking about relationship. *What's your relationship with Jesus?*"

I held my breath. No one had ever pressed Howard face-to-face about Jesus.

Although he'd received the baptism in the Holy Spirit, he hadn't seemed to move further in his relationship with the Lord. Howard's experience of God was still mainly in his head, not his heart.

Dick's question triggered a deep fear in Howard that he had reacted to in sarcasm many times in the past, and he voiced it again now.

"What do you want me to be, a psalm singer?" Howard shifted uncomfortably. "I'm not going to be like one of these guys who go around looking pious. That's not for me."

"I understand where you are," Dick answered.

Little did Howard know at the time, that Dick had the same abhorrence for phoniness and pretended piety as Howard did. So did Jesus. But Jesus would not be thwarted by the fear that had a strangle hold on one tall, blond travel agent's heart. He would keep reaching out.

Dick turned back to me and posed a question I was to hear more than once: "Why do you want Howard to change, Jane?"

POINTS OF CHANGE

His question pushed me at a sensitive point. The answer seemed self-evident.

"What is marriage, anyway, if it isn't two people meeting each other's needs? Even the Bible talks about husbands loving their wives like Christ loved the church."

I could explain my point of view, but I couldn't explain what was happening to me; things were beginning to crumble inside. Dick's question, "Why do you want Howard to change?" kept reverberating through my mind.

Now, for days after our counseling sessions, I felt weak and vulnerable, as if something inside me was giving way. Like the patient in the operating room, it was my turn for heart repair.

UNCOVERING WRONG BELIEFS

After several sessions with Dick and Marilyn, I began to notice a pattern in how Dick confronted me. It closely resembled the stance of a prosecuting attorney in court.

"Jane," he said, "you believe your husband should love you in the way you want to be loved. When he doesn't, you become self-protective and angry."

Pow! My head spun. I'd come to Dick and Marilyn to present my case and here I was being treated as if I were the guilty one.

Before I could defend myself, Dick continued. "Doesn't God's word say, 'Whoever hates his brother is walking in darkness'? How can you say that you have a relationship with God when you hate your brother? After all, your relationship with your brother is only a picture of your relationship with God."

Everything in me wanted to marshal a verbal army of convincing words to defend myself. I'd never before had this belief buffeted by Scripture—without room for exceptions. "Isn't it true, Jane, that Jesus said we were to lay down our lives for our brother?"

"But I have," I protested. "I've encouraged Howard to communicate. I've kept a good house, paid the bills, gardened, kept up the yard. . . ." I paused for breath. "I've done everything I could to keep things going at home."

Dick's response came back like a fast ball. "Well, that's not necessarily laying down your life. That's doing 'things' for people and still keeping your real self closed and distanced from them."

I found myself bristling.

Surely I knew something about Scripture. I'd been raised in a pastor's home and attended Sunday School faithfully ever since I could remember. Furthermore, since my experience with the Holy Spirit, I'd been devouring Scripture, often for hours a day.

Still, I was being challenged left and right. I could identify with the poor defendant scrambling to justify his actions as Dick pointed out, one by one, that my beliefs didn't line up with what the Bible said.

"When the Bible says, 'What you sow, you reap,' that applies to anger," Dick explained. "Jane, if you sow anger, you'll reap anger."

My response was instant. "But that doesn't feel fair. Howard's not doing his part. He has some responsibility in this marriage, too." I could feel the blood rush to my face and my fist tighten in my lap.

"Indeed, he does," Dick nodded. "The call on the man's life is clearly stated in Scripture: he is to be the priest of the home. But remember, no one can make him fulfill his side of the marriage contract. And, at the same time, his failure doesn't excuse you from loving him."

Finally, I looked at Dick and sighed. "You sure go for

the throat, don't you?" He let my comment stand as if he hadn't heard me.

Then Marilyn spoke up. "Jane, often when we read the word, we read the man's part where it outlines the husband's responsibility. You need to remember that we are responsible before God for only our part.

"The fact is that Scripture is unequivocal at this point. That's what Jesus taught in the Sermon on the Mount: Believers are called to love and walk in fellowship with our brothers and sisters, even when they do not love in return." *

I grew limp. This was more than a little debate. This was the cross at work, slashing through my rights, my self-protection, my sense of fairness, my me-centered agenda. Love when you are not loved in return? Love in the midst of pain? This would call us to an impossible task. The very thought of it felt like death.

TRUTH IN THE SILENCE

Neither Dick nor Marilyn said another word. We sat in silence. It was obvious the counseling session was over for the day. I had plenty to think about.

Just as I stood to reach for my coat, Dick made one last comment: "By the way, Jane, I don't go for the throat. I go for the heart."

For the first time since we'd come to counseling, Howard and I drove home in total silence. I, who always noticed the towering evergreens along the winding road above Puget Sound, made no mention of the fresh green tips of

---

* I'm not suggesting that a woman in an abusive situation remain in that circumstance. She should seek the help of a counselor or pastor qualified in abuse counseling.

spring's new growth. We didn't even stop at McDonald's for our usual cup of coffee.

Within minutes of pulling into our driveway, Howard scooted up the stairs to read the newspaper. I headed straight for my bedside Bible and brought it to the kitchen table. I had to see for myself what Scripture said about love.

I opened to the book of First John. The words stood out on the page like neon signs, heralding descriptions of God's love. I'd read all these verses many times, but they'd never impacted me like this.

Through the counseling process, I was seeing, not only the anger but the hatred in my own heart. Now, with my heart open and willing to look at and admit honestly what was really there, the truth of the Scriptures was coming alive to me in a new way.

I read and wept and wept and read.

Revelation. Enlightenment. Scales falling from my eyes.

I was seeing truth; it was reaching me at the heart level. The contrast of light and darkness was unmistakable. "Anyone who claims to be in the light but hates his brother is still in the darkness" (I John 2:9). Relationship! The concept permeated every chapter. "Anyone who hates his brother is a murderer, and you know that no murderer has eternal life in him" (I John 3:15). No compromises, no exceptions in this passage. "If anyone says, 'I love God,' yet hates his brother, he is a liar" (I John 4:19).

These weren't wishy-washy words or mealy-mouthed phrases. They were strong, definitive, and absolute. *Hater. Murderer. Liar.*

Here I was, reading about the one basic of the Christian faith—love—and, because I was honestly opening my heart, I saw myself in a new light: I was totally wrong. "Whoever does not love does not know God, because God is love" (I John 4:8). Nothing here was contingent on the other person's loving me in return.

Dick's words haunted me: "Why do you want Howard to change?" I knew the case was ended. My defense was demolished.

MOMENT OF TRUTH

An epic moment of truth surfaced, one I will never forget. Now I knew the answer to Dick's question, but the words stuck in my throat. I hated to speak them, even in the quiet of my kitchen.

Why did I want Howard to change? My head bent, my heart open, I whispered, "For me! For me! For me! To meet my needs. For my happiness." I wanted change, not for Howard or even for God, but for Jane.

For the first time in my life, I saw the depth of my own sin, my own desperate need for change.

"It's me, O Lord, standing in the need of prayer. Not my brother, not my sister, but me."

As painful as the counseling process was, I would no longer resist the scalpel of truth.

The next time the four of us met, I gave Dick and Marilyn complete freedom. "Hold back nothing," I said. "Leave no stone unturned. Tell me the truth. I want to be free."

Although Howard was apparently not as in touch with his pain as I was with mine at that point, he was willing to continue our counseling.

CUTTING DEEPER

Dick's and Marilyn's goal in counseling was to help me identify what I actually believed. This "battering on beliefs" had to be the starting point, because we live our lives out of what we hold to be true in our hearts.

110

It is not what we think or know in our minds, but what our hearts are convinced of that directs and guides our lives.

We all build our lives on premises, beliefs that we form, and that "work" for us. These may be ideas we've learned in school, at home, or even ones we've "caught" unconsciously as children from those we look up to. Sometimes, they're wordless expressions: a look on a face, an attitude shown in a situation, but they help form our beliefs.

Brick by brick, we bring these beliefs into our impressionable minds, building the foundation from which we live our lives.

Our behavior will give evidence that some of our heart-held beliefs are wrong. We accept them as true and they are not. Is it any wonder we eventually run amuck in our relationships, with God, and with those around us?

Dick kept probing at my flawed heart, ferreting out the wrong beliefs I'd based my life on and exposing the angry responses that subsequently followed.

Sometimes the scalpel of his words hit the artery of self-righteousness called *pride*, and I would begin to bleed. Then Marilyn would come alongside and clarify the direction we were going.

"Jane," she asked one day, "what do you get when you squeeze an orange?"

An obvious question, I thought.

She pursued her illustration. "You get orange juice because that's what's inside the orange. In your relationship with Howard, you are being squeezed. And what comes out of you? Anger!"

For an instant, my heart sank again. Who wouldn't get angry? But before I could protest, Dick picked up Marilyn's point.

"Howard can't make you angry, Jane. No one has that kind of control over another person. Your feelings are *your* feelings. They are a barometer of what you believe in your heart, and that's what's causing your distress.

"It's a sin problem, Jane."

That word again. Exactly the lesson I had begun to learn at the kitchen table recently. Dick leaned back in his chair, giving opportunity for his words to sink in. I could feel the Master Surgeon at work, "dividing soul and spirit, joints and marrow" (Heb 4:12).

SURGERY'S SUCCESS

Remarkably, during the next weeks at home, the Holy Spirit seemed to have a new kind of access to me. He expanded, clarified, and confirmed in the Bible where I had missed the truth.

One day, Jesus' words in Matthew 15 gripped me with a startling awareness of my condition: " 'But what comes out of the mouth comes from the heart, and this is what makes a man unclean and defiles [him]. For out of the heart come evil thoughts (reasoning and disputings and designs) such as murder, adultery, sexual vice, theft, false witnessing, slander, and irreverent speech. These are what make a man unclean and defile [him]' " (vv. 18-20).

I had never thought that what was spewing out of me—my boiling anger—was not only being unlovingly poured out on Howard, it was turning back to poison me in the process.

Slowly, like the layers of an onion, my wrong beliefs, my anger, and self-protection began to be painfully stripped away. I could see for myself that my behavior was under-written with my own sinful strategies. My attention had been taken off what I perceived as Howard's deficiencies, and the spotlight was now shining with glaring intensity on what was in my heart.

No wonder the Bible gives strong words of admonition

in Proverbs: "Pay attention to what I say; listen carefully to my words. Do not let them escape out of your sight, keep them within your heart, for they are life to those who find them and health to a man's whole body" (v. 4:20).

No wonder Jesus said, "'Man does not live on bread alone, but on every word that comes from the mouth of God'" (Matt. 4:4).

INTENSIVE CARE

My eyes, and my heart, were being opened to a staggering reality: The Bible was not an inspired book of how-to's for errant children. It was a love letter about relationships: God's with us and ours with God and others.

I saw now that my whole self-protective approach to life affected my relationships with virtually everyone. Nothing in my life, however, had ever exposed my wrong belief more clearly than my relationship with Howard.

My whole approach to life and to marriage was 180 degrees from God's plan.

Mine was self-serving, unloving, and unscriptural. At the core, I had come into marriage to get, not to give. Yes, change was needed; I was right about that. But the only person I could change was me.

This could be no mere outward adjustment. I was embarking on a journey to discover what real love was. Up to this point in my life, I'd taken some wrong roads, but they had only sidetracked me. The truth is, there are no short-cuts or detours with God. When you have walked in wrong beliefs as long as I had, you don't change overnight. It takes time to learn a new way.

In the ensuing days and weeks, the Spirit of Truth continued to expose the attitudes in my heart. It was a veritable "stripping down" of my old beliefs as I weighed them against God's Word.

Inside a Woman

In his letters to the church in Ephesus, Paul writes about putting "off the old self" and putting "on the new." The passage speaks of growth in a graphic way: "You were taught with regard to your former way of life, to put off your old self, which is being corrupted by its deceitful desires. . . . to put on the new self, created to be like God in true righteousness and holiness" (Eph. 4:22-24).

Paul picks up the same idea of taking off the old and putting on the new in his letter to the Colossians. In both instances, the Greek words for *taking off* mean "disrobing," such as taking off an old coat.

Initially, I had come to Dick and Marilyn for help because my "old coat" was no longer adequate, and I thought I'd walk away wearing a "new coat."

But I was discovering that I needed more than a simple wardrobe change. I needed the Holy Spirit and the Word of God to radically realign my heart beliefs. In addition, I needed God's empowering grace to enable me to keep putting "on the new."

Radical? Yes.

But God's antidote for sin is nothing short of radical.

His truth would not only be His instrument of healing, it would be my constant companion on the journey to love.

7
...
Thirsty Pilgrims

The relentless rays of the midday sun beat down across my shoulders. I dug into my purse for dark glasses and another squeeze of suntan lotion to smooth over my arms and dab across my forehead. All morning I'd looked forward to this stop on our Holy Land tour: Jacob's Well, one of the most authenticated sites in all of Israel.

I was in Jerusalem. On this particular day I was with a group touring the high spots of biblical history—and relishing every minute of it! From the blustery boat ride across the Sea of Galilee between Tiberias and Capernaum, to the solemn sharing of the Lord's Supper at the Garden Tomb, I was falling in love with this little country.

I couldn't take it all in fast enough—the gentle, rolling hills, the peaceful green valleys, the dusty roads, the little towns, and the teeming city of Jerusalem. My mind savored every historical tidbit the tour guide gave as he painted word pictures of life in Bible times.

But while my mind was soaking up the facts, my heart was melting. There was more here than just a little country of rocky fields, shrines, and archeological digs. There was more here than just being in the historical center of our Judeo/Christian heritage.

This place pulsated with life! And I knew I wasn't the first to feel it.

God's life was here in some inexplicable deep dimension, transcending all of history and every culture and throbbing with His passionate heartbeat for His world.

That afternoon, the temperature hovered around 85 degrees in the Samaritan town of Nablus. "Come on, everybody. I know it's hot, but you need to see this site up close." The tour guide herded his busload of wilted tourists out of the air-conditioned coach, across the street, and over to the dirt courtyard inside the ruins of an unfinished Greek Orthodox church.

My footsteps sent dust puffs ballooning into the air. Some so high they tickled my dry throat into an immediate sneeze. "This is the only well in the area that has been in continual use since the days of the patriarchs." The eager tour guide couldn't wait to tell us more. I leaned forward to catch his words, but I sneezed once more and missed half of his second sentence.

I rummaged back into my purse, this time for my handkerchief. Too late to block another sneeze. I again heard only a portion of what our guide was saying. Something about this being the spot where Jesus met the Samaritan woman and asked her for a drink of water.

AN EMPTY JAR AND AN EMPTY HEART

Jesus. The Samaritan woman. My mind leapt backward to the familiar scene by Jacob's well, described so clearly in John's Gospel:

Jesus, tired as He was from the journey, sat down by the well. It was about the sixth hour. When a Samaritan woman came to draw water, Jesus said to her, "Will you give Me a drink?" (His disciples had gone into the town to buy food.) The Samaritan woman said to Him, "You are a Jew and I am a Samaritan woman. How can You ask me for a drink?" (For Jews do not associate with Samaritans.) Jesus answered her, "If you knew the gift of God and who it is that asks you for a drink, you would have asked Him and He would have given you living water" (John 4:6-10).

Even as I stood there in the hot sun mentally replaying the story, I was struck with the parallel between the woman with her water jar and myself.

In 2000 years, the issue here hadn't changed; it was still thirst.

How well I knew it as my own dry throat clamored for relief.

"How about a drink from Jacob's Well?"

I thought he'd never ask! But he did. Our tour guide knelt down at the top of the well and turned the crank that brought up the cool, refreshing water. One at a time he dipped out mini-cupfuls to us, sun-baked tourists with parched throats. My turn couldn't come quickly enough. I was thirsty!

So was the Samaritan woman whom Jesus met at the well. Yet her need went far deeper than mere physical

117

thirst. And Jesus knew it. Filled with His Father's compassion, He looked beyond her promiscuous lifestyle, and saw her heart, dry and barren, and thirsting for love.

Here they were, just the two of them alone at the well. One skeptical, tentative woman, desperately needing answers for her life. And Jesus, full of grace and truth, with *the* answer. Gently, but directly, He extended His offer: *Living Water* to quench the thirst in her heart.

We know the rest of the story. The Samaritan woman naively interpreted Jesus' gift of living water in the contemporary language of the Jew. To them, *living* water meant *running* water.[1] She knew the water of Jacob's well had only percolated from the subsoil; it didn't bubble up from a free-flowing stream. Where would Jesus have access to running water? His offer, she thought, bordered on blasphemy. Was He saying that He was somehow greater than Jacob who had dug this well for his family and his cattle?

Quickly, however, her curiosity exceeded her questions. Although perhaps still skeptical, she reached out for what He had to offer. " 'Sir, give me this water so I won't get thirsty and have to keep coming here to draw water' " (John 4:15).

Jesus brought the verbal byplay to a close and told the woman to call her husband to join them at the well. With that one directive, her lifestyle was exposed. Yet, strangely, she didn't turn and run. " 'I have no husband,' she replied" (John 4:17).

Seeing her openness, Jesus moved on to confront her gently with the facts of her relationships: None of the five men she'd lived with was her husband, including the current one.

How could Jesus have known about her past? Was He a prophet? Quickly she put two and two together and questioned Jesus who directly identified Himself as the Messiah.

SHE HAD VALUE

Such an astounding disclosure brought everything into place for this thirsty woman. At last! She'd found what she'd been searching for all her life: love and acceptance. Here was One who knew all about *her*—yet He fully accepted her. In His eyes, she had value—as a woman, as a Samaritan, and even as a sinner. Perhaps for the first time in her life she experienced love that overruled judgmental superiority. Her response? She opened her heart.

No longer bound by shame or her outcast status, she rushed back into town, leaving her water jar sitting in the dust by the well! The whole town must know about this Man who " 'told me everything I ever did' " (John 4:39).

John records her one-woman evangelism thrust simply. "Many of the Samaritans from the town believed in Him because of the woman's testimony" (John 4:39). Doesn't that say something about the depth of human thirst when this kind of news pushes past people's long-standing cultural antagonisms and sends them running toward the well with empty cups?

BACK HOES AND JACK HAMMERS AT WORK

My physical thirst had been wonderfully assuaged that hot November afternoon at Jacob's Well. I'd also been deeply moved at rethinking the story of Jesus' tender love toward the Samaritan woman. I had a lot more in common with this woman than wanting water. Sure our strategies differed, but we were both thirsty for the same thing—someone to love us. We just went about pursuing "thirst quenchers" in different ways. Foolish ways.

She sought for love and meaning in her life through her long string of relationships with men. I took a different tack, but in a way I was pursuing exactly what the woman at

119

the well was after: security, the feeling of being loved, and having significance, the sense of having value.

While my approach was more socially correct, it was, nevertheless, the same: self-relating. I wanted to get these needs for security and significance met from my perfect performance as a wife and homemaker and from another person—Howard.

When I returned from Israel and began counseling again with Dick and Marilyn Williamson, this was the exact place they brought me to in an early session. "Jane, you are trying to get your needs met in Howard." We must have come back to this statement a dozen or more times before there was even a crack of light in my understanding.

My boiling anger was the tip-off. I was angry because all my attempts and strategies to get my needs met had failed.

"Change will come," Marilyn encouraged, "but it will take time to look at some of the heart beliefs you've held. Particularly the one that says you can get your needs met apart from God. That's the tough one, the core belief of what the Bible calls 'foolishness.'"

These counseling sessions with Marilyn and Dick were, without a doubt, some of the most productive, life-giving hours of my entire life. I was meeting with two people whose demeanor and patience exuded Jesus' love and caring and who were dedicated to helping me take responsibility for my reaction to the hurts of the past and set me free to love, even in the midst of pain. At the time, however, the sessions were often hard. At other times glorious breakthroughs brought me to new ground.

To begin with, as *my* beliefs were hammered down by the clear teaching of the word of God, I encountered emotional pain such as I'd never known. My way of thinking about life, about myself, about my marriage, even about God was challenged on every front. I've equated the process to heart surgery, but there were times when it also felt more like a gigantic remodeling project with back hoes and jack hammers having free rein to every corner of my life—with me in the middle cowering without a hard hat!

My thoughts and feelings took the full force of the construction project under way. Sometimes bruised and battered, other times pushed to the joy of new freedom—my emotions had no choice but to roll with the program. I'd sit down at the kitchen table to read the Bible and journal in my notebook, write a few words, then collapse in tears over the pain of my self-centered approach, the way I'd lied to myself, or my lack of love toward Howard. Sometimes I'd veer off course by justifying my actions, but then I'd flinch at my obvious self-righteousness.

At other times, I spewed out anger as my long-stuffed feelings of resentment gushed to the surface, surprising even me with their intensity. Through it all, Scripture became my plumb line; I recounted what had been said to me and then systematically dove into the Bible to clarify what I was hearing from God's Word. It was all progress, but I confess that many days I was certain I was riding a fast train backwards—destination: death, not life.

Bit by bit, however, truth was getting through to my heart. The truth of God's Word as I was being faced with it was getting through, as well as the truth the Holy Spirit was unfolding to me personally, particularly on the issue of *foolishness*.

UNCOVERING FOOLISHNESS

"When we try to get our needs for security and significance met apart from God, we always go to foolishness."

Dick's statement seemed clear, but I couldn't fathom what he meant. "Go to foolishness?" The phrase had no more meaning to me than "go to Chicago or New York."

121

But the Williamsons followed up their statements with Scripture, verses I'd often read before but never grasped as being life-changing words. At the close of one session, Dick and Marilyn said their goodbyes and then Dick smiled and reminded me to meditate on Proverbs 22:15.

"Foolishness is bound in the heart of a child" (KJV). That particular proverb led me to a totally new understanding, not only of my role in our marriage, but my entire approach to life!

Foolishness. We are born with it. That's basically what "bound in the heart of a child" means. Our sin nature is bent on going our way, not God's. The word *bound* means "under compulsion." It is the inclination of our hearts. It may sound strong, but the truth is, we—everyone of us— are born determined to go our own ways.

And what is this foolishness that rules us? In his basic seminar, Dr. Larry Crabb defines it as "a conviction that life can be found apart from God." In his book *Inside Out* he goes on to say, "We long for a life that is real, full, and happy. We think we can make this kind of life happen so we take things into our own hands to try to make it take place."[2]

The inevitable fallout of this man-centered, self-directed, foolish life plan is that we develop into empty, lonely people. Our lives become disordered and racked with anxiety. We have broken marriages and sickness because our ways don't satisfy those needs of ours that are designed to be filled by our Creator. As we know, this development is nothing new; the history of God's covenant people is riddled with stories of their stubborn determination to go their own way and how God faithfully— and repeatedly—sent His messengers to call them back to Him. Listen, for instance, to the prophet, Isaiah, as he echoes this familiar cry of God's heart toward His people:

This is what the Lord says—your Redeemer, the Holy One of Israel: "I am the Lord your God, who teaches you what is best for you. If only you had paid attention to My commands, your peace would have been like a river, your righteousness like the waves of the sea" (48:17, 18).

We don't have to look far to see evidence of this same destructive path all around us. Sadly, even among people who adamantly declare that their life and joy is found in the Lord Jesus, we see behavior that shows they really don't believe this in their hearts.

I have been to retreats where women, caught up in the beautiful flow of the Holy Spirit, can sing, "Jesus is all I need." Yet, they've told me later that as the retreat goes on they are able to identify areas of foolishness in their own lives where they look to things and people to fill the emptiness they feel inside them. In the actual experience of their Christian walk, they live as if Jesus is not all they need. There's a big gap between their confession and reality.

Ever since man swallowed Satan's first lie in the Garden of Eden, we have easily been seduced away from godly thinking. Look for a moment on some of the foolish ideas that we buy into, substituting the world's wisdom over God's wisdom.

• Money makes a man important.

• Living in the right house or neighborhood will establish me as an important person.

• If my husband loved me in the way I need and want, I could be fulfilled and happy as a woman.

• If I could find the right mate, I could be complete.

• If I could earn a college degree, I'd feel important among my peers.

• If I could attain the right weight, I'd feel attractive

and acceptable as a woman.

• If I had enough money in the bank, I'd be secure.

Sounds like a contemporary list, doesn't it? However, the prophet Jeremiah might well have taken the same inventory in his day as he proclaimed God's Word to the Israelites: "'My people have committed two sins. They have forsaken Me, the spring of Living Water, and have dug their own cisterns, broken cisterns that cannot hold water'" (Jer. 2:13). The driving human thirst for security and significance is timeless—as are the foolish beliefs that propel us to meet these needs apart from God through our own strategies.

Although both men and women have these basic God-given needs, men's stronger need is for significance, women's for security. Yet both set goals that they feel must be accomplished in order to have these needs met.

A man measures his significance by his position in life, his success on the job, or the amount of money he earns. While a woman, looking for security, turns to people, to her home, her career, or her appearance to meet her needs.

An excruciating event when Howard and I were first married illustrates one of my foolish beliefs to gain acceptance through my outward appearance. When Lisa was just a baby, Howard and I flew to Hawaii for a travel convention. One night we were to attend a special dinner party, one of those social "command performances" where there is no alternative, but to "be there."

On a limited budget, I wore a simple cotton dress I'd made and to which I'd added a few matching accessories, thinking I'd be comfortably appropriate for the evening.

Never in my wildest dreams was I prepared for the bucket of insecurity that splashed over me as I walked in the door of the hotel's sumptuous dining room. My first thought was that we'd stumbled into the wrong room, that, by mistake, we'd walked into the governor's inaugural ball. The sight of all these people dressed so elegantly nearly took my breath away.

The women looked like they came straight out of the pages of *Vogue*. I saw one wearing an iridescent blue silk sheath, and another woman in a shimmering white sequin suit. They were all expensively dressed—designer clothes with complimentary jewelry—and their hair perfectly coiffed. Even their perfume filled the room with exclusive scents. I stood there feeling like Cinderella after midnight, standing at an exquisite ball dressed in her Simplicity Pattern #4682. I wanted to crawl back home, curl up in my jeans, and eat a TV dinner.

Instead, I grabbed for my lifeline—Howard. He took my hand, introduced me to some of his co-workers, got me a glass of coke, and then left me with one of the wives as he moved across the room to talk and laugh with his friends in the travel business. "Is this your first time in Hawaii?" Val, a lovely fortyish woman in a soft beige angora beaded sweater and matching silk dress, twirled the straw in her ice tea and looked up at me with a pleasant smile. Even her small talk sounded smooth and interesting.

But, my mouth went dry, as if it were filled with cotton candy. I took a long sip of my coke before I could even answer, "Well, yes, this is my first time here. Howard's been before." (That sounds so dumb, Jane. Can't you think of anything more exciting to talk about?)

But I couldn't. And the animated conversation going on around me only reinforced my negative critique. I couldn't think of what to say, how to act, or what to do. Except for one thing: to feel hurt and angry at Howard. Why wasn't he standing by my side, giving me the moral support and confidence I needed to survive this awkward social situation?

THE BLAME GAME

Blaming someone else. That reaction comes automatically when pain strikes. But blame is only a smoke screen covering the insecurity in one's heart. Howard wasn't the problem, I was. Me and my own sense of inferiority that kept nipping at my heels like a persistent puppy. At that moment, under the elegant chandeliers and standing by the dazzling hors d'oeuvres table, I felt as though the whole room was shouting, "See, Jane, you don't measure up." But in reality, the room was mute; the negative message I heard came from inside me.

As I looked toward Howard, I could feel the anger and demandingness rise in me. That's the progression foolishness takes—a wrong belief that others will meet our needs. Then, gradually a demand that they *must* meet them. When they don't, anger and resentment jump on the band wagon and a full scale parade marches destructively through our hearts.

How grateful I am that some thirty years after this dinner party, God rained on that little parade. He rained love and hope and forgiveness—and even more. He Himself came to march through my heart. Where I'd looked to people, things, appearances to fill up the emptiness I felt inside, where I'd projected an image that I thought would bring me acceptance and love, He came with the quiet, but certain truth that I was acceptable just as I was.

IT'S OKAY TO BE THIRSTY

Dr. Larry Crabb describes our plight as thirsty pilgrims. "We long for both respect and involvement, impact and relationship. In the desert of a fallen world, our soul is parched."[3] He goes on to say, "Every fallen person created to enjoy God is thirsty."[4]

126

Stop right there; that's the catch! We are thirsty for what we were created for—relationships. First with God, the One whose image we bear, and then with those around us. Wanting and needing love is a legitimate part of our make-up. Our humanness.

Why does God tell us over and over again in the Scriptures that He loves us? Why does He command us to love Him and others? (See Matthew 22:37-39). Why?

Because He made us that way.

He made us for relationship—to thirst for Him and to be richly nourished by the love of others. We need Him as we need the very air we breathe.

This side of heaven, we're all thirsty people longing for the security and significance we lost at the Fall. And it's okay to be thirsty. Jesus never chastised the Samaritan woman for having legitimate longings. Neither was there anything wrong with my longing to be loved. Our problem lay in what we did to assuage our thirst—our self-centered strategies, our self-protection, and lack of godly love.

My friend, Connie, tells what she did with the thirst in her heart. She denied it even existed. Coming from a broken home as a little girl of seven to live with an older aunt and uncle, she survived emotionally by becoming a high achiever and a people pleaser. Her strategy worked well into adulthood, until a few years ago when a problem cropped up in her family.

She made an appointment to talk with a pastor about the situation. Almost immediately the adept pastor sensed where he could really help Connie. He asked her if she felt her aunt and uncle loved her. Without thinking, she responded, "They did the best they could, but they were farmers, busy people, you know."

The pastor faced her directly. "Don't you believe little girls need love?" She couldn't answer. He pressed her

127

Inside a Woman

further. "I'd like you to say, 'I am a person who needs love.' " Such a simple request, but the words stuck in her throat as she tried to say them.

"I felt humiliated and horribly uncomfortable," she remembers. "It was all I could do to repeat the words. But I said them, 'I am a person who needs love.' "

For years, Connie had denied her God-given thirst for love. Her lack was too painful to look at. If she faced it, there was the very real possibility in her mind that she just might be unlovable. Without feeling loved, she had only one alternative—to live her life believing she didn't need any. So she did. She lived a "nice" life—distancing herself emotionally behind a self-protective wall.

Unfortunately, the lie she believed soon gave birth to another: that she was not acceptable as she was. An emotionally deprived child, she then set about vigorously meeting her needs on her own terms.

In her case, she pushed herself to achieve academically; from childhood through college, she drove herself to be first in every competition that came along. After all, there were always rewards to allay her sense of lack. Gold stars, applause, certificates, and blue ribbons—these pathetic trophies became the substitutes for the love she really wanted.

If Connie had somehow been present at the Feast of Tabernacles when Jesus taught at the temple courts, she would have known it was okay to be thirsty.

Do you remember that wonderful scene on the last day of the Feast? In our day, we'd say Jesus was in hot water; the pressure was on among the chief priests and Pharisees to silence this rabble-rouser—once and for all.

But Jesus was not about to be still. He stood up and in a loud voice said, " 'If anyone is thirsty, let him come to Me and drink' " (John 7:37). He didn't say, "If you're thirsty, ignore it, deny it, stuff your feelings, compensate in some

128

other way." No, He said, "If you're thirsty, COME!"

And He's still giving that same invitation today. It's okay to be thirsty. In fact, it's wonderful and blessed to be thirsty (See Matthew 5:6)—but come, get water. Not just a cupful, but life-giving rivers of living water that will quench your thirst and flow out to others in eternal dimensions.

AN APPETITE FOR WISDOM

When I was growing up, we often kidded about being members of the "clean plate club." My brother Jimmy and I were no exceptions to a common mealtime expectation of children in the '40s and '50s. "Eat whatever is put before you. If you don't like spinach or peas, you will when you get hungry enough."

My dad often took that illustration to the spiritual realm. He used to say, "If you go hungry long enough, you will gain an appetite for things in God you would not normally desire or seek after."

Looking back, I believe that this is precisely what God was allowing for me. He was wanting to show me what was in my heart—the foolish beliefs and empty pursuits that would not satisfy. It felt like a desert place, not unlike the wilderness he led his covenant people through.

"You shall remember all the ways which the Lord your God has led you in the wilderness these forty years, that He might humble you, testing you to know what was in your heart, whether you would keep His commandments. And He humbled you and let you go hungry, and fed you with manna which you did not know, nor did your fathers that He might make you understand that man does not live by bread alone, but man lives by everything that proceeds out of the mouth of the Lord" (Deut. 8:2, 3 NAS).

Inside a Woman

The Lord in His love for us allows our hunger and lack of satisfaction to intensify to a point where we begin to realize the emptiness of our barren pursuit at the same time our hearts and appetites are being awakened for God. He is the only one from whom we can draw life. Every other strategy is foolish. But where is the way out? What will turn us around?

There is only one thing: living our lives by godly wisdom. This is the direct opposite of living by human wisdom, which is foolishness before God.

"Get wisdom, get understanding; do not forget my words or swerve from them" (Prov. 4:5). Like manna in the wilderness, God's Word would feed my malnourished understanding and turn me from my man-centered orientation. Oh, how I needed that word which would be "a lamp to my feet and a light for my path" (Ps. 119:105). scripture after scripture began pointing me to the unequivocal wisdom of God and the absolute necessity of living by it.

"The fear of the Lord is the beginning of knowledge, but fools despise wisdom and discipline" (Prov. 1:7). Whether it was the collapse of a house foolishly "built on sand" (Luke 6:49) or fools eating "the fruit of their ways" (Prov. 1:31), there were consequences when one chose not to live by God's Word. And conversely there were benefits when one did; a house that stands when the storms hit (Luke 6:48) and being safe "from the ways of wicked men" (Prov. 2:12).

I'd had enough of foolishness, the junk food of life.

I was tired of going my own way. I was hungry to be nourished with the bread and meat of wisdom and thirsty for the water that would satisfy.

CHANGING BELIEFS

Do you know what it feels like to begin a physical fitness regimen? To cut back on the fat grams and empty calories and to plunge ahead with a vigorous exercise program? To me it spells "long haul, upward road, sweat and tears." Results won't come overnight. And it will take effort.

I felt that way often when Marilyn and Dick challenged my beliefs. I'd come to counseling to change Howard, and I'd been brought face-to-face with my need to change, not my husband, but myself.

Knowing the truth, however, is always the beginning point of freedom. From that place, I could move toward the remedy which would bring the wholeness I needed so desperately.

Changing false beliefs is a path without shortcuts, a process that lets us begin to line up our lives with the Word of God. It is absolutely essential.

If our beliefs are incorrect, our whole life will be built on a wrong foundation. The Apostle Paul knew what he was talking about when he said that the way to being transformed is by "the renewing of your mind" (Rom. 12:2).

Let me summarize some practical, biblical steps I learned in this process of changing wrong beliefs:
Remember:
1. Admit what you believe in your heart.
   - When there are recurring negative feelings, find the unbiblical pattern you are following. There is a root problem you need to identify.
   - Deal with the root problem rather than rehashing the same old feelings and issues. God wants us to be reconciled and to let go of the lie once and for all.

131

2. Confess what you believe. (To yourself, to the Lord, to others.)

3. Repent of your belief. (Compare your belief with the Scriptures—How does it compare with godly beliefs?)
- Repent for coming against God's Word. Many people weep over their pain, but not their sin. Repentance is essential. From the Greek word *metanoia*, repentance means to turn around and go another direction.
- Own your action as sin against God.
- Make a deliberate decision to turn from it.

4. Ask the Lord's forgiveness. "Lord I am totally wrong. Please forgive me for putting my truth before the Truth."

5. Receive His forgiveness. The biggest problem we have is to allow ourselves to be forgiven. We feel we must be punished or pay.
- Choose to receive God's love and cleansing and forgive yourself.

6. Walk in the new belief. (Line up your beliefs to the Word of God. "I am totally wrong, Lord, you are totally right.")
- Let the Word of God continue to be the basis for your new belief.

There will be many tendrils attached to the roots of our false beliefs. We will see the harm our false—or ungodly—beliefs have done to us. As this happens, ask the Lord to totally forgive you for that false belief that has harmed you so. And He will.

Walking in God's truth is much like planting a garden. Seed will go into the ground. It will need to be watered while you wait for it to grow. God's word will not return empty (Isa. 55:11), and the Holy Spirit will be there to bring it to life.

COME AND DRINK

True, I'd been a stumbling, thirsty pilgrim, looking for life in all the wrong places, believing the wrong things. But the same Jesus who met the Samaritan woman at the well also had water for my parched soul. From the barren wilderness of Palestine, before Christ, from the hot sands of Egypt, from the dusty villages of Jesus' day, to the bleak, hopeless desert places of our lives, God still offers life-giving water to thirsty pilgrims.

" 'Come, all you who are thirsty, come to the waters; and you who have no money, come' " (Isa. 55:1).

8
...
Out of Hiding

I did not learn to walk in the fullness of God's truth overnight. Instead, it was a process of replacing my wrong beliefs one by one and then taking my first steps like a child learning to walk. God in his wonderfully creative way used other people and a variety of situations to teach me.

One day, I learned something important about myself during a casual lunch.

Bill, his wife Marilyn, Howard, and I were laughing and chatting together over seafood salads when I made an insignificant remark. Bill cocked his head and chuckled before he spoke, "Jane, you're like a private country club."

I put down my glass of water and did a double take. A private country club? These words came from a man whose opinion I respected and who, I felt, knew me well. Howard and I had spent together with Bill and Marilyn.

"Bill, what on earth do you mean?" I asked.

He smiled, and answered in a gently teasing tone, "Only a few get in, Jane."

His observation jolted me. Was I some kind of a snob? I loved people; surely he couldn't accuse me of being exclusive.

Funny, isn't it, how we view ourselves? I never thought of myself as being a "closed" person. Reserved, quiet, that's how I would have described my personality. Being the life of the party was outside my comfort zone, but I saw myself as warm and friendly.

Yet I couldn't ignore Bill's comment. Was he saying I was a closed person?

Immediately, I had a mental picture of a palatial clubhouse, fronted by massive white pillars, surrounded by acres of perfectly-edged lawn. Flowers were everywhere, set in nursery-perfect rows. It was the kind of private club you see in movies where you drive down a long narrow road blocked by an imposing gate. When you stop, you have to pass a litmus test to prove you belong. The comparison unsettled me.

FACING THE ISSUE OF OPENNESS

The country club issue didn't go away.

Sometime later in a counseling session, Dick and Marilyn asked me to share my growing up days with them.

When I got to the crisis in my parents' marriage during those traumatic days in Glendale, Dick stopped me. "We need to look at how you reacted here, Jane. You were afraid, a little girl feeling like her world is falling apart in front of her, and, of course, you had a reaction."

Dick paused for a moment to search my face before he

My Growing-Up Years

Wagon riding with my adored older brother, Jimmy.

At age 13, I had a frizzy perm, hand-me-down clothes, parents on loan to everyone else and a borrowed bike.

By high school I earned a pair of popular Spalding shoes and cashmere sweaters by working part-time.

Branches From My Family Tree

My red-headed mother
Mystel, a talented musician.

Aunt
Ina
always
had a
hug
for me.

Great Grandmother
Burson's kitchen was a
place of comfort and
good cooking.

My parents, Tom and Mystel
Williamson, used their musical
talents often for church services.

From Parsonages to My Own Home

My husband, Howard, with Jeff and Lisa in our little red house.

Jeff and I on the front porch of "little red."

Our parsonage in Akron, Ohio.

Our California Years

Howard and
I with Lisa,
Scott, and
big brother
Jeff.

My '60s "California Girl"
image included blond
hair, frosted lipstick and
flower-power prints.

A Family Celebration

Scott's wedding to Jody in 1989 brought us all joy. (From left) Lisa's husband, Bob; Lisa, Jane, Jody, Scott, Howard, Jeff and his Stephanie as flower girl.

Our Next Generation

Our grandchildren (l to r), Olivia, Valerie, Stephanie, Amy Austin, and Michael.

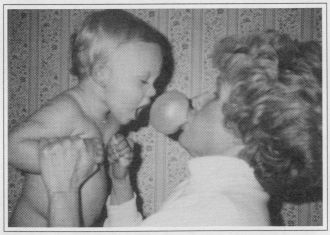

Austin and I share a bubble at bath time.

Aglow Around The World

Below, our daughter Lisa's first baby was born during the 1987 Int'l Conference at New Orleans; they surprised us with pictures!

Above, demilitarized Jane and Howard in Korea, 1992.

At the 1990 National Conference in Washington, D.C. (From left) our pastor and his wife, Dick, Marilyn Williamson; Howard, Jane; Aglow staffers Dee Fink, Pat Gaines.

Our Journey Goes On With Joy!

Howard and I in 1958, courting in a '57 Chevy convertible.

*Howard and I in 1992, out of hiding,
knowing forgiveness, walking in love.*

continued soberly. "When you vowed that no man would ever hurt you like your father hurt your mother, you closed emotionally."

Closed? That word again. I looked across the table, puzzled. Do people open and close like swinging doors? The concept was still new to me. But from then on, we began dealing with other points in my childhood that had also contributed to many decisions that I had made to close my heart.

Yet even at this stage, I wondered why Dick and Marilyn were making such an issue about openness. What was wrong with being reserved, with not speaking your mind every time? It still seemed to me that complete openness was a goal of questionable worth that might hold more trauma than deliverance.

When I took this issue before the Lord, however, He showed me in Scripture where openness was always in His plan and why it was vital to my healing.

GOD'S PERFECT PLAN

From the beginning, God had a plan. His plan was to have a family, a people, a race, a nation through whom He might reveal Himself. As the doors of time open, we hear these words: "'Let us make man in Our Image, in Our Likeness'" (Gen.1:26). We see this first in the Garden of Eden with Adam and Eve.

The word, *image*, according to *Strong's Concordance*, means "representative figure." Think about this in terms of the story of Adam and Eve. The very one God created would himself represent God on earth. He (and all who followed him) would be the family God wanted, the people who would express His life to the world. The vehicle for all of this would be relationship.

Yes, relationship would be the key. God's plan was that

the world would see His people's love for Him and then how that love was expressed in relationship with one another.

They would see God's people work through difficulties in relational matters with openness, love, forgiveness, and mercy and recognize that God's Kingdom was being expressed in their midst.

PARADISE LOST

In God's garden paradise, Adam enjoyed unclouded fellowship with God. No tension. No distancing. No walls to stop the natural flow of love and fellowship between them. Complete openness.

No walls, that is, until sin entered with its terrible consequences.

Even before Adam's sin, God's plan was brutally attacked. Lucifer (Satan) rose up against God. He rebelled against the Ruler of the Universe, wanting to exalt himself above the most high God. He wanted two things: preeminence, the opposite of humility, and independence, the opposite of dependence, which is an ingredient of relationship with God and others. In his craving to be first, he struck a blow at relationships, for it was through relationships that God would reveal Himself in the earth.

Since the time of the Fall, we, too, seek those two qualities, preeminence and independence. We want preeminence in relationships. We also seek to maintain independence and self-protection rather than dependency and the giving of ourselves, and those acts of our will fight with the very purpose God has for relationships.

Beginning with Adam and Eve, man became separated from God, from those around him.

Adam not only ran to hide, he tried to cover himself as well. But his Creator/Father was fast on his heels, His tender cry resounding across paradise, " 'Where are you?' "

(Gen. 3:9). Adam's incredibly revealing answer followed, " 'I heard you in the garden, and I was afraid because I was naked; so I hid' " (Gen. 3:10).

Fear propels us to self-preservation.

Ashamed of his nakedness, stricken by his failure, fearing exposure, Adam turned away from God. For him, it was the only escape he knew: hiddenness. Then, fearing rejection, he covered his body with fig leaves and his heart with a shield of fear. What he was created for—fellowship with God—was broken.

Man closed his heart.

Fear and shame as well as hurt are ingredients of closedness.

Pastor and author, Dr. A.W. Tozer, wrote about these issues.

> Hardly anything reveals so well the fear and uncertainty among men as the length to which they will go to hide their true selves from each other and even from their own eyes. Almost all men live from childhood to death behind a semi-opaque curtain, coming out briefly only when forced by some emotional shock and then retreating as quickly as possible into hiding again. The result of this life-long dissimulation is that people rarely know their neighbors for what they really are, and worse than that, the camouflage is so successful that they do not know themselves either."[1]

SATAN'S ATTACK ON RELATIONSHIPS

We need to know unequivocally that Satan's whole agenda is diametrically opposed to openness and humility, the stance God calls for in maintaining loving relationships with Himself and others. Satan's insidious assault is always directed against relationships.

But it's not primarily our relationships that Satan is after, it's God's plan. Satan attacks relationships as a means to the end and in the end, it's God that Satan is after, always. So if the enemy can cause us to falter in the area of relationships, can cause us to close our hearts to one another, he succeeds in defaming the image of God to the world. We are left with no testimony.

Satan continues to this day to wreak havoc in our hearts with his press for preeminence and independence. His old refrain has never varied: Be independent of God; seek life on your own terms.

GOD'S RELATIONSHIP BASICS

Jesus is emphatic on this issue of relationship as it affects the unity among believers. We hear it clearly in His high priestly prayer:

"My prayer is not for them alone. I pray also for those who will believe in Me through their message, that all of them may be one, Father, just as You are in Me and I am in You" (John 17:20).

It is not unity for the sake of cozy togetherness: it is unity with an eternal purpose. "'May they be brought to complete unity to let the world know that You sent Me and have loved them even as You have loved Me'" (John 17:23).

Clearly, the whole gospel is built on relationships, open relationships. Everything we do in our Christian walk is built on relationship with God and then with others. Let me enumerate:

• We begin our life in Christ with a relationship. This covenanted relationship with Jesus is foundational for all other relationships.

• The Ten Commandments deal with relationships. The first four with God, the last six with one another.

• Marriage is to be lived out in the context of relationship, with true commitment, true companionship, and true communion.

• Parenting is built on relationship.

• The Body of Christ is relational in nature.

Edith Schaeffer, interviewed in *Focus on the Family* magazine speaks to the crucial issue of relationships in families. "There is art work to be done in relationships. Fifty years of love and appreciation do not come in a package with the marriage vows."[2]

Schaeffer is bringing openness into the flawed, human parts of family relationships when she suggests that a mother explain to her children, "I'm not perfect, your dad isn't perfect, none of us is perfect. We're just a lot of imperfect people living under the same roof for just a limited number of years. But the reward of continuity in family life is worth working for."[3]

Her description is a beautiful picture of the family of God, the Body of Christ, as it is on earth: I'm not perfect, you're not perfect, none of us is perfect. We're a lot of imperfect people living under one covering. But God in His infinite wisdom knew that the plan of having a family in the earth would best fulfill His purpose. For Himself, for humankind, and ultimately in the countering of Satan's rule in this age called time.

The church (God's family) is made up of people who are not whole because of Adam's sin. Jesus Himself made this quite clear: " 'It is not the healthy who need a doctor, but the sick. . . . For I have not come to call the righteous, but sinners' " (Matt. 9:12, 13).

We need to remember that we came to Jesus not all put together, but all undone. We came in need of a Savior/

physician. The church, in one sense of the word, is a hospital, a place where those in need of restoration, the imperfect, the hurting, the wounded can come to be loved, accepted, encouraged, and helped towards wholeness. This will only happen as we are healed in the area of our relationships. And the first step in that direction is learning to be open people.

THE ANATOMY OF OPENNESS

How do we get back to the openness man experienced before the Fall?

My adventure toward openness started with a decision I made at my kitchen table. When I finally saw how all my relationships were stalemated at a surface level, I chose to open up my heart. That's the first step: making a choice to be open.

Webster's Dictionary defines openness as: "A state which permits unobstructed entrance or exit. Not closed, not covered, clogged or shut. A state which permits freedom of view. Not enclosed, fenced in, sheltered, or covered over. A lack of pretense. Expanded, as an open book."

Let's continue to look at what openness is:

• It is more of an attitude than an action.

• It is a feeling we give other people that we are willing to share our hearts, our real selves down inside without fear.

• It is a willingness to be known.

• It is a willingness to risk disclosing ourselves which always brings with it the risk of being misunderstood, criticized, hurt, rejected, or judged. But because we are growing in our capacity to trust God and His love for us, we are willing to trust ourselves to one another.

Honesty and truthfulness are critical in our pursuit of God. The psalmist asks, "Lord, who may dwell in Your sanctuary? Who may live on Your holy hill?" (Ps. 15:1).

See how the psalmist answers the question of how to be near God: "He who walks uprightly, and works righteousness, and speaks the truth in his heart" (Ps. 15:2 NKJ).

The real key to both relationship with God and with others is in our necessity to speak truth in our own hearts. To be honest with ourselves about ourselves.

When we are open and honest with God, our "closedness" that kept His love from being felt is now removed. Love can flow in and love can flow out. Only then are we in a position to be open on the horizontal level; our hearts are protected by God's love and we can risk being open to those around us. Love now has a chance.

HIDING IS CLOSING

Let's take a look at the other side of the issue.

Hiding emotionally compares to the child's game of hide-and-seek. You dart out of sight, find a secret place, and when someone comes looking for you, you remain breathlessly still, out of their sight. Your goal is to stay so well hidden, you are never seen or caught.

Like Adam, I tried to conceal my imperfections in hopes that I could keep the real truth about me from others. I lived with a pervasive sense of unacceptability to others and judgments against myself.

Not only did I hide the "real Jane," I presented the world with another Jane, one of my own making and one I'd gotten quite comfortable with.

Pastor David Seamands, in his book *Healing for Damaged Emotions*, aptly describes this same path I took— from hiddenness to projecting an image.

Somewhere in the process of growing up, the child receives messages about himself, about God, about people, and about relationships. These messages can be taught or caught. They can come through what is directly said or done, or what is not said or not done . . . The child who has received negative messages then knows: "I am not accepted and loved as I am. I've tried every way to get this approval by being the way I am. Now I can only be accepted and loved if I become something else and someone else."[4]

PSEUDO JANE

Shortly after bringing up the issue of my being closed, Dick and Marilyn lovingly identified this pseudo Jane. I'd learned at a young age that people can be critical, judgmental, and hurtful. As a sensitive child who perceived she was unacceptable, I could not risk being vulnerable to people. That risk terrified me. In order to survive, I felt I had to make myself acceptable, to carve out another Jane to present to the world.

Dr. Seamands goes on to shed light on this familiar human process:

The youngster doesn't sit down and figure this all out . . . Some very necessary feelings never come across to him, feelings like security, acceptance, belongingness, and value. His need to be loved and to learn to give love is not met. Instead there develops a growing deep anxiety, and feelings of insecurity, unworthiness, and undesirableness. And the youngster begins to climb the long, torturous trail of trying to become someone else.[5]

How subtle, yet how grievous the transition is from what Dr. Seamands calls the "real you" to the "super you." According to him, "The super you is a false idealized image you think you have to be in order to be loved and accepted."[6]

As superwoman I didn't fly through the air in a blue cape or soar over skyscrapers. I flew around inside myself, in an attempt to be perfect. I was the one who must do it right, say it right, look right, and never smudge my mascara.

My false strategy was brought to light and challenged as I sat at Dick's and Marilyn's table.

Dick posed a hard question to me: "Jane, what if everything that surrounds you was stripped away from you—husband, children, your home, your possessions, your position, ministry, finances, clothes?

"What if it were all gone? What would be left? Who is the real person inside? Do you believe that you need all these peripheral things to make you acceptable?"

What do you say to a challenge that specific? It was sobering. I who hated phoniness was seeing that in my desire to be acceptable, I had, without knowing it, become less than real. Part of me wanted to run for the nearest fig leaf outlet store.

But I knew through this journey that the Lord was pressing me for good.

GRAVEN IMAGES

After our counseling session, I drove toward home, jarred by the directness of Dick's question and, at the same time, motivated to discover my honest answer.

The miles sped by while I considered what I'd just learned. At the same time, I subconsciously noted the billboards, the little tugs plying up Union Slough off Puget Sound, the pulp mill chimneys of Everett puffing out white smoke—all the sights I knew so well on this route.

Into this emotional/geographical potpourri, the Holy Spirit dropped two little words: *graven image*. I chuckled

145

aloud. What a God! He doesn't waste any time; He talks to His kids right in the middle of a busy freeway.

I found the reference right away that evening after dinner, hunched over the kitchen table with my Bible, my dictionary, and my coffee. "Thou shalt not make thee any graven image" (Deut. 5:8 KJV).

Graven image. The dictionary brought clarity.

Graven means something carved out or sculpted. *Image* means an imitation or representation. The golden calf the Israelites made in Moses' absence is a good illustration: a lifeless, powerless, man-made object of worship. God's word is inalterably clear on graven images. But I confess to have viewed this commandment solely in the context of pagans in unchristianized lands.

Now it was speaking to me with a contemporary—and personal—ring.

God wanted me to put away my idea of what a super mother should be, what a wife should be, a leader should be. I would have to pull down my image of what I thought others expected me to be.

Here again, Dr. Tozer's words underscored the crucial nature of the issue at stake. "Self-knowledge is so critically important to us in our pursuit of God and His right—eousness that we lie under heavy obligation to do immediately whatever is necessary to remove the disguise and permit our real selves to be known."[7]

Once more, my kitchen table became the scene of Kingdom business. I reread the scripture from Deuteronomy and confessed my sin of erecting a graven image—a false projection of myself. Now I could see it as a sin against the Lord and others. I repented for going my own way and made a decision to be an open person.

For the first time in my life, I was willing to be known for who and what I was.

THE REAL JANE

Change is rarely comfortable. In those next few weeks and months, I often felt out of control. I even had some fears that I would feel naked without my familiar cover-up. But I continued to fight years of ingrained habits and wrong reactions and soon I made some extraordinary discoveries that gradually erased my fears.

People were responding to the real Jane. At work, people mentioned that my face looked less strained, that I seemed more at ease, more approachable. I'd hear, "What's happened to you, Jane?" I couldn't always give a clear explanation except to say that God was at work. More than anything, I was aware of a growing love for those around me and a freedom to express that love.

BEGINNING A REAL MARRIAGE RELATIONSHIP

God was also at work in our home. As my self-protection came off and I started sharing the real Jane with Howard, he began to feel safe in our relationship in a way that allowed him to share the real Howard with me.

We started walking together in the mornings along the Edmonds waterfront, above the ferry landing where we had a full view across Puget Sound to the rugged Olympic Mountains in the west. Somehow our pleasure at this awesome sight doubled when it was shared.

Often on these walks, Howard and I talked about the ordinary mundane things in our lives, when we should trade in our car or how we could update our kitchen. Sometimes we shared the deep secrets of our hearts, asking for forgiveness or praying for each other and our family. We prayed for Aglow, the nations, and the current world situation.

We savored every moment, from the first step along the bluff above the water to our little finale in the Scandinavian bakery where we had coffee and split a muffin before we returned to our busy schedules.

Openness, we were discovering, was the stuff of our new relationship. It was so good just to be ourselves among all the flurry of the harbor activity, sea gulls included.

And that's an irony worth noting. For here below the noisy, squabbling seagulls, our hearts, once so injured and distant, were discovering a new bond of love and peace. Seagulls, after all, are no match for lovebirds!

GOD'S WORD IS TRUE

Howard and I were so busy enjoying each other's company, we hardly noticed that the transition in our marriage was happening right under our noses. Intimacy and closeness, the feelings I'd struggled so hard to pound into our marriage, were being felt by both of us as a new, rich love flourished. God worked in our lives in ways I never imagined.

Why are we always surprised at the truth of God's Word? It provides practical, day-to-day, gutsy-living reality simple enough to understand.

THE ADVOCATE OF OPENNESS

Jesus always advocated realness and openness. Look at the way he welcomed little children. He loved their vulnerability. " 'Let the little children come to Me and do not hinder them, for the kingdom of heaven belongs to such as these' " (Matt. 19:14).

He even went so far as to say that the childlike stance was a prerequisite for getting to God in the first place. " 'I tell you the truth, unless you change and become like little

children, you will never enter the kingdom of heaven'"
(Matt. 18:3).

OPENNESS ON WHEELS

Let me share with you a recent experience with openness I witnessed in my own front yard.

One Saturday I'd gotten up early to attack the weeds that sneaked between our azaleas and rhododendrons. As I worked my way around the plants, I heard an unmistakable noise.

Looking up I saw three little boys riding their bikes up our cul de sac for all they were worth. Their infectious laughter gave the weeds in front of me a reprieve as I stopped to watch the boisterous trio crisscrossing the street. Hilarity dressed in jeans. Adventure in high gear.

"Hey, guys, watch me!" One zig-zagged across the street and abruptly skidded out a figure eight as he braked to stop.

"That's nothing, look at this!" The tallest boy pulled rank over his younger friends, pedaled like crazy, and hung a wheelie that earned him their immediate respect.

"Wow!" the others chorused, stopping for a brief second before they pumped their way back up to the crest of the hill.

Suddenly, the littlest boy, pumping behind them screeched to a halt and yelled, "Hey, everybody. Stop." As if under military orders, the others braked and turned around. When he had their full attention, he addressed them with dead earnestness:

"Hey, you guys . . . do you like me?" The clear, poignant question filtered out across the street with all the innocence of a naked toddler streaking through the house after his bath. I put down my trowel and leaned forward.

The older boy looked at his young friend for a second

and answered emphatically, "Sure we like you." "Yeah, we like you," echoed the other boy. No hesitation. No snickers. No laughter.

Issue resolved. The contented boy mounted his bike again and together they rode off to the crest of the hill.

"Do you like me?"

I thought about this question posed without a shred of embarrassment as I bagged up the weeds and carried them to the garbage can. The little boy asked outright what his heart honestly wanted to know. His openness gripped me.

When I mentioned it to Howard at dinner that evening, we began to speculate about a comparable adult scenario.

"Imagine a chief executive officer of an international corporation suddenly getting up from the board room table and addressing his directors, 'Excuse me, but I have to ask you a really important question. . . .'" I began to laugh.

Howard jumped in, chuckling. "They'd put down their Mark Cross pens, stare at the man in his custom-tailored suit and wait expectantly for something profound."

We could see the whole scene unfold: The executive's question followed by awkward silence, nervous glances. Would any of those directors stand up and congratulate him for his honesty? Not on your life!

Because the world says it's not okay to open up your heart like that. It's weak. It's one thing for an eight-year-old boy in jeans and tennis shoes to be honest, but a grown man? The world tells him he's foolish.

THE UNCOMFORTABLE QUESTION

You see, there's more here than an honest question. The reason the executive's question would make them so uncomfortable was because it would touch their own self-protection. It would finger the places where these men and women long ago had learned to hide the real person inside them. His transparency would make them feel embarrassed to admit their own need for love and acceptance.

Suppose, for instance, that genuine honesty spread through the board room after that question. Suppose that the executive vice-president stood up, cleared her throat and said, "Yes, I like you, and furthermore, I respect your honesty. But now I need to know something . . . do you like me?"

Then maybe, just maybe, some brave soul would jump to his feet and confess, "There's a hole inside my heart so big, I feel it can never be filled up. But I've been afraid to tell you how empty I feel."

Most of us know only too well those same feelings whether the setting is in a corporate skyscraper, a church pew, or at the family dinner table. How many times have we been part of a group or social gathering, aching on the inside but wearing a smiley mask on the outside?

The same mask that we think protects us also imprisons the knot of emptiness inside and prevents others from seeing our real selves.

THE MASK OF SELF-PROTECTION

Protection has its positive aspects. God created us with a built-in security system. When we are threatened physically or emotionally, we instinctively react to protect ourselves from harm.

We have neither tortoise shell nor a skunk's offensive spray as a shield, but we do have inborn defense mechanisms to protect against pain. Whether it is the surge of adrenaline that carries us through an accident or the blinking of an eye to wash away dust, we can be grateful to our Creator for this healthy aspect of self-protection.

However, the negative side to our protective strategies was what I was beginning to see in myself.

Inside a Woman

I could never have skidded my bike to a stop and asked my friends, "Hey, do you like me?" I couldn't risk being myself when that self didn't feel valued.

We protect ourselves in dozens of ways from being exposed or known and thus remain closed people. Allow me to share some of the major behaviors we use as protection:

- We use anger in two ways . . . to put people off, and to stay away from our own pain.
- We can use laughter to hide our real feelings, and stay in surface relationships.
- We can use talkativeness or quietness as a way of staying hidden.
- We can use intellectualism displayed by a superior attitude or lofy speech to distance ourselves from others.
- We use flirting as surface behavior that puts off real relationship.
- We use a need to be right to cover the flawed real self inside.

By adulthood, I'd wrapped myself like a mummy in my own self- protective strategies. But I was totally unaware that I'd moved to a dishonest lifestyle, closed to those around me and not giving them access to the real Jane. My mask was glued in place, projecting respectability and an I've-got-it-all-together image.

Perfectionism is self-oriented and self-gratifying. In short, it is worldly behavior.

Instead of becoming vulnerable sinners in need of God's grace and the cleansing power of Jesus' blood, we become performance oriented. And that is not a ticket to Kingdom living on a train called The Grace and Mercy Express!

Here's the good news: For every detour sinful man takes, God offers a U-turn toward Kingdom living. He alone holds the map to bring us out of hiding, back to where the living is free, where love flows, and relationship is rich and satisfying.

Let me tell you about one of those turnaround experiences I had when God's truth touched me—literally.

I attended the World Map Camp Meeting in Penticton, British Columbia, Canada. Following the meeting, Jack Hayford, senior pastor of Church on the Way in California, looked at me and said, "I feel I need to pray for you before you leave." He kneeled beside my chair, praying quietly in the Spirit. With tears in his eyes, he said to me, "I feel that the Lord is telling me to peel a mask off of your face." I felt him touch my cheek as he began the motion of peeling off a covering over my countenance. He began at the chin, then up over my cheeks, my eyes, and finally over my forehead.

At the time, I knew something profound was happening. This man of God, under guidance from the Holy Spirit, foreshadowed perfectly what the Lord would do in me during the next few years.

The facade that covered my face was being peeled off in preparation for a new work of God.

THE OPEN-HEARTED CHURCH

Larry Crabb encourages believers to make the commitment to openness. "The Church needs leaders who can involve themselves in other people's lives with the joy of integrity and transparency, confident that their love is unfeigned, willing to be deeply known for the sake of helping others."[8]

But a word of caution. In this age of "anything goes," we need to approach openness with godly wisdom. Openness is not telling everybody everything at any time for no reason. Openness is not license, it is an attitude of the heart.

Inside a Woman

Because it is an attitude of the heart—a feeling of openness that comes from me—there is an availability to my heart that was not there before, a willingness to share my heart out of a motive of love and commitment to helping others in their pursuit of God.

When we become more committed to becoming the person God created us to be rather than protecting the person we have pretended to be, we will find our way out of hiding, into openness, and more fully into the purpose of God. But that requires humble confession, repentance, and a choice to seek God's face at every turn.

9
...

The Face of Forgiveness

If you've had kids, my guess is that you've also had: mud tracked in on the living room carpet, a window broken from a stray baseball, and perhaps a car fender dented when your novice driver made a solo run to the grocery store. As Edith Schaeffer said about families, "We're a lot of imperfect people living under the same roof."[1] Sometimes we rub more than just shoulders; we rub each other the wrong way.

Everyone expects a few rough spots when we relate to people, whether it's in a family, in a job, at school, or even at church. Maybe it's an upset over something as minor as missing a dental appointment or forgetting to take a phone message. Falling in the category of minor "bumps" on the road of life, these incidents are usually quickly dismissed with a casual, "Oh, you're forgiven; forget it. It's okay."

What is harder to dismiss, however, is the aching sting of a deep personal hurt that continues to generate inner turmoil. It has penetrated so deeply you wonder if you will be scarred forever. Sometimes the pain is so tangibly present, you're convinced it has lodged permanently in the lining of your heart, where, unknown to anyone but you, it silently bleeds your life away.

I relate to that kind of pain. For years my personal diagnosis could well have been charted: "Undealt with pain. Bruised. Tender. Internal bleeding."

Perhaps for you, it was a recent event when harsh words or a trusted friend's betrayal caught you unaware, delivering an unexpected blow from behind. It could have been that a family member verbally assaulted you or even sexually abused you. As a result you may feel deeply humiliated and devalued as a person. Or maybe you came from a "good" family. You lacked nothing materially, but, at the same time, you never received the nurturing love and affirmation you needed as a child. Your empty heart yearned for love and acceptance and when you did not get it, you grew up with an emotional void inside. To this day you carry the ache of that deprivation.

In these situations our response isn't as simple as, "Forget it. It's okay." This isn't like getting mud on the carpet. We can't just phone the rug cleaners in the morning and have them remove the pain by afternoon.

A PICTURE OF PAIN

Let me tell you about my friend, Julie. The youngest of twelve children, she was born into a poor, but warm and loving, Kentucky family. Her mother died when she was six months old, her father when she was two. For a time, her sisters struggled valiantly to keep the family together, but eventually Julie was placed in a foster home.

Not just one foster home, but a succession of them. Good, solid homes, most of them Christian, where Julie received loving care. Still, it wasn't the same as being in her own family, and Julie grew up feeling like an outsider, like she didn't really belong. Typical of children in similar situations, she found a way to compensate for her insecurity: she became a "good little girl," always on her best behavior for fear of being sent away—again.

Eager to learn, Julie did well in school, and wanting to be a teacher, enrolled in a Christian college. Here she met Ross, the son of missionaries, also studying to become a teacher. They had the same values, the same faith, the same interests in art, history, and travel. Not surprisingly, they fell in love and were married shortly after graduation.

The rest followed in story book sequence: teaching jobs, a lovely first home, two wonderful little boys, and opportunities to serve in their church, Ross as an elder and Julie a Sunday School teacher. In addition, she led a Good News Club in her home, a Christian outreach for the neighborhood children.

Life was good for Julie; she had found the security she always wanted. It came wrapped up in a husband who loved her, two children to nurture, and a home of her own.

Then without warning, her world caved in.

As he'd done every morning of their married life, Ross kissed Julie goodbye on his way out the door to school. However, when he returned home that evening, he did not kiss her. Instead, he walked into the kitchen, paced nervously for a few minutes, reached for a glass of water, swallowed a few mouthfuls, and turned to face his wife. "I no longer love you, Julie," he blurted out. "I love my secretary. And I want a divorce."

Stunned that her husband of twenty years had been

having an affair, and that he chose to leave his wife and family for another woman, Julie plunged into the deepest emotional turmoil of her life. As if pierced by a dagger, her heart beat with the wound of rejection and betrayal, even to the point of suicide.

Fear gripped her. How would she ever marshal enough strength to support her boys, eight and fifteen, as they wrestled with the devastation in their lives? For Julie this would not be one night's bad dream; the upheaval in her life evolved into a ten-year nightmare.

More than once she felt like a rag doll that had been carelessly tossed to the side of the road. Left in a dust heap, no longer "special" to the one she'd entrusted her heart to. Dealing simultaneously with rejection, loneliness, lack of money, and eventually both sons on drugs and alcohol, there were days when she feared her little home, once the safe harbor for a happy family and the gathering spot of the Good News Club, would never again be filled with joy and laughter.

To compound Julie's pain, Ross, now remarried and settled across town in a new condo, was busily boating, traveling—and ignoring his sons. His carefree, affluent lifestyle poured salt on Julie's open wounds.

A STAIN ON THE HEART

Can you imagine the bitterness that would enter in the wake of such devastation? Here was Julie, caught in a series of excruciating events she neither asked for nor had any control over. She was the innocent victim of another's self-centered choices.

Whatever the outside source, emotional pain like Julie's invariably lodges in the heart. Undealt with, it remains like a stubborn stain in the fabric of our lives, coloring everything we do with its sorrowful tinge. Even more destructively, it prompts us to close our hearts in self-protection, building walls—between us and God and between us and those around us.

Sadly, this kind of penetrating pain rarely goes away on its own. It doesn't don its hat one day, wave goodbye, and walk away whistling down the street. No, unnoticed it burrows underground where it quietly fuels anger and resentment, then surfaces when something or someone else triggers it again. Neither innocent nor dormant, it has the potential of locking us in prisons of bitterness for years.

Just ask "Dear Abby." In response to one of her recent syndicated columns on forgiveness, she was deluged with letters describing how hatred and bitterness robbed people of years of rich relationships. One woman confessed: "I had an older brother who had given me genuine cause to hate him since I was twelve years old. I am now seventy-five." Another woman wrote: "I have spent at least thirty of my forty-two years hating my mother."[2]

What help is there for dealing with this kind of pain, for the people locked in bitterness, for the Julies of this world, so wounded by unfair treatment? What help for victims of abuse? What recourse is there for those suffering painful childhood hurts, like mine, passed on from well-meaning parents who did not love in a way their children found fulfilling? Where is the way out of these painful prisons?

The Bible is clear: there *is* help for those incarcerated by such woundedness. Listen to Jesus' own words: "'The Spirit of the Lord is on Me, because He has anointed Me to preach good news to the poor. He has sent Me to proclaim freedom for the prisoners'" (Luke 4:18). And again, in the Old Testament picture of the Messiah: "He has sent Me to bind up the brokenhearted, to proclaim freedom for the captives" (Isa. 61:1). Jesus Himself is the help. Yes, He holds in His hands the key that will unlock the doors of our emotional prisons. He has paid dearly for it.

Look closely at His nail-scarred hands. Do you see the key? It's stamped: Forgiveness.

Jesus identifies with our pain. He Himself wept over Jerusalem, wept at the death of His friend, Lazarus. We know He hurt. He was "a man of sorrows and acquainted with grief" (Isa. 53:3 KJV). And He knows we hurt. "For we do not have a high priest who is unable to sympathize with our weaknesses" (Heb. 4:15).

Here He is, the Son of Man, relating to our frailty. His father-heart cannot bear to leave us closed and locked behind bars of self-protection when we fail to deal with the hurts in our lives. Too wounded to receive His redemptive love, we stand empty-handed, with nothing to share with others. However, God is at hand, loving and accepting us in our pain and wanting to rescue us from its trap.

Yet Satan wants us ensnared and he tempts us at this very point to stay in our bitterness.

Strong's Concordance defines temptation as "an enticement to sin." That's precisely Satan's strategy when it comes to our hurts, our resentment. In any way he can, he entices us to remain in our pain and bitterness. And above all, not to see it as sin. He wants to deceive us into shrouding our wounds with a cape of respectability, perhaps to honor ourselves with a badge of recognition: Victim of the Year.

Can't you hear Satan's negative line: "These little emotions are mere nothings. Just deny them. They don't begin to compare with the BIG SINS, adultery or murder. Besides, after what happened to you, you have a right to feel the way you do."

If we fall for the enemy's line, we play right into his hand. His strategy is to immobilize us by causing us to harden our hearts. If he can do that, then he can frustrate God's master plan for the whole world, which is nothing less than expressing His love through His believers.

A WAY OF ESCAPE

The Good News is that we don't have to be stuck with blind eyes and hard hearts; we can move beyond the place of the pain and bitterness. Why? Because God has provided a way of escape.

Listen closely to the Father's heart through the encouraging words of the Apostle Paul. "No temptation has overtaken you but such as is common to man; and God is faithful, who will not allow you to be tempted beyond what you are able. But with the temptation will provide the way of escape also, that you will be able to endure it" (1 Cor. 10:13 NAS).

Essentially Paul is pointing out two things here: first, that we are tempted. That's a fact. And second, that God has made an escape for us in every temptation. That's the hope.

Once more *Strong's Concordance* helps clarify. It cites the word *escape* as meaning "foot." Yes, as surely as God made a way through the wilderness, He has made a way for us. Centuries ago as Joshua stood hesitantly outside the Promised Land, God encouraged him with a powerful promise: "'I will give you every place where you set your *foot* as I promised Moses'" (Josh. 1:3).

Hear the depth of those words. They are our marching orders even today! God is in essence saying to us, "I want to give you dominion over the enemy in your life. I want you to walk victoriously in your land. Even as Joshua could walk victoriously in his land, even as he could push his enemies aside and take possession of what I had promised him, so can you." God has given us authority over the things that cause our feet to stumble and our hearts to hurt.

He has given us a way to walk out of our hurts and wounds. His way of escape? Forgiveness.

But he involves *us* in the process. He honors our will. We must make the choice to accept his way.

FORGIVENESS ISN'T EASY

Forgiving others is not easy. Someone has said that it is love's toughest work and love's biggest risk. The act itself is simple, but because hurts occur within a storm of complex emotions, we rarely feel like doing it. Think about it! Who really feels like forgiving someone who has inflicted pain in his life? Who feels like being vulnerable when she's been the recipient of an unfair act? After all, if you've had a brush with a porcupine, you don't turn around and embrace the creature!

In her book *Something More* Catherine Marshall underscores this concept. "The love God demands can only be the gift of God. Yet He cannot give us that gift so long as bitterness and resentment have slammed shut the door of the heart and unforgiveness stands sentinel at the door lest love open and enter. Forgiveness is God's precondition to love."[3]

Most of us would chose to run the other way, find a place to lick our wounds, and stay closed to those who hurt us. We might plot how we can get even. And then if we hear a story such as Julie's we want to shout, "Hey, wait a minute. This is unfair and unkind. We need justice here."

For years I made that same protest. "I've done everything I can do to make this marriage work. Howard needs to do something." Convinced that I was the innocent party, I believed he was the cause of my pain. So, in my hurt, I closed my heart to Howard and lived longer than I care to remember with pain and unforgiveness churning inside me.

Let's face it, forgiveness is not an automatic human reaction. The whole world says: "Find out who's guilty and make him pay." We want that person to hurt as deeply as he has hurt us. We can even want revenge.

Revenge? Yes, this reaction in natural man is as instinctive as breathing. Hurt? Injured? Then, strike back. Get even. Punish.

The Old Testament Mosaic covenant dealt with this aspect of human nature, even codifying the reaction specifically: "Fracture for fracture, eye for eye, tooth for tooth. As he has injured the other, so he is to be injured" (Lev. 24:20). On the surface this sounds like a mandate for retaliation, but it wasn't.

In the ancient Near East, the practice was to kill the one who had caused injury. Thus, the Law of Moses, which sounds vindictive on the surface, actually was aimed at limiting brutality to a manageable scope, not encouraging retribution.

By New Testament times, the Pharisees interpreted the law to mean that if a person injured another, he had to pay compensation equivalent to the damages caused.[4]

KNOWING GOD'S HEART

And then Jesus bursts upon the scene with a ministry showing what real love and forgiveness is all about. And it is not about law; it is about relationship.

Relationship. Jesus shows us throughout His teaching and preaching that this is what is on the Father's heart. Relationship is always the key with God.

That's why forgiveness is such a critical issue. For unforgiveness held in our hearts always blocks our relationship with God. And when that relationship is blocked, all our relationships are affected.

Listen for this emphasis so clearly underscored in Jesus'

teaching on the grassy hillside above the Sea of Galilee near Capernaum.

Easy breezes sail off the water and up through the little knolls, moderating the temperature of an otherwise hot afternoon. The twelve, that inner circle of disciples, sit tightly wedged in the "front row seats," even leaning toward Him so as not to miss any words their beloved Master speaks. But there is a wider audience as well, others intent on hearing what this itinerant preacher has to say.

Like a good rabbi, Jesus sits down to teach. He begins referring to the laws they're so familiar with. But within minutes, their heads are swimming with questions: "What kind of an approach is this?"

"'You have heard that it was said . . . "Do not murder, and anyone who murders will be subject to judgment." But I tell you that anyone who is angry with his brother will be subject to judgment'" (Matt. 5:21, 22).

"Angry? But come on, that's just a garden-variety everyday emotion. Everybody gets mad once in awhile." Puzzled looks are exchanged, some clearing of throats, a little elbowing, and lots of muttering.

Jesus, however, keeps on talking. "'If you are offering your gift at the altar and there remember that your brother has something against you, leave your gift there in front of the altar. First go and be reconciled to your brother; then come and offer your gift'" (Matt. 5:23, 24). Heads bob back in shock and comments fly. "This is ridiculous. If someone's hurt you, it's up to them to make the first move to reconcile."

For those so schooled in the rigors and traditions of the Law, Jesus' words must have sounded like impossible gibberish. But His aim was neither to confuse them nor to give an innovative twist to the laws they already knew.

164

He came wanting to show them one thing: the Father's heart of love. This was a love that impacted others with genuine mercy and heartfelt forgiveness. A love that brought life and healing in relationships. That nourished and built up.

This was the message of the Kingdom of God. The Pharisees had majored in the "outward" while God was calling for "the inward." Not law, form, and traditions, but love, mercy, and grace for relationships.

The gist of Jesus' teaching was revolutionary to his hearers: "Go deeper than what the law says. Pray for your enemies; don't kill them. Forgive those who hurt you; don't seek revenge. Watch how I eat with taxpayers and sinners. You go out and do the same. Break out of your legalistic straight-jackets. Throw open the doors of your hearts and love!"

FORGIVENESS WITHOUT HOOKS

God's priority as expressed by Jesus is undeniably clear. Listen again to His commandment: " 'Love the Lord your God with all your heart and with all your soul and with all your mind. This is the first and greatest commandment. And the second is like it: Love your neighbor as yourself. All the Law and the Prophets hang on these two commandments' " (Matt. 22:37-40).

God's heart is for love and forgiveness without hooks: a giving with no expectation of getting anything back. No exceptions. No shortcuts. No qualifiers. We are left with a mandate to produce nothing short of unconditional love and forgiveness.

But how do you do this if you're like Julie, deeply wounded by her husband's unfair treatment? Or if you've been beaten and absent from your family for several years like Terry Waite, Anglican envoy, or Terry Anderson, the

165

American journalist, or any of the other hostages held captive so long in Beirut?

How do you forgive those well-meaning parents, who in their inability to love well, caused painful hurts? Those others who abused, even brutalized you?

What is the answer?

We seem to be between a rock and a hard place.

On one hand, Scripture leaves no loopholes in admonishing us to forgive: "'And when you stand praying, if you hold anything against anyone, forgive him, so that your Father in heaven may forgive you your sins'" (Mark 11:25).

On the other hand, within ourselves, we don't have what it takes to leap over the hurdles of our hurts and offer forgiveness. Has God really called us to an impossible task?

Yes! Without a doubt. We are called to do something we cannot do. And, like the Israelites, whom God allowed to be humbled and proved in the wilderness, the sooner we know the depth of our inability to forgive the better.

THE WORK OF GOD

I still remember one day following counseling when that impelling awareness hit me full bore as I sat with my Bible, again at the kitchen table. God was pressing me about the issue of forgiveness and, undeniably, I had a ways to go. I read and reread and cross-referenced scriptures that spoke of forgiveness, many of them very familiar passages. I saw others with new clarity and focus—and imperative. And there at my table I literally raised my hand in surrender. My poor-me, unforgiving attitude plainly did not align itself with the Word of God.

Sure, during our counseling, my relationship with Howard was growing stronger and more open all the time, but when he answered me too abruptly or lost his temper over what I thought was "nothing," it was like I hit the brakes. Edges of the old anger crept back in; I reached for my old scorecard of his failures.

I didn't always move forward and forgive him. My heart told me I should, but I didn't; I withdrew, waiting and hoping Howard would come and apologize to me first. I wasn't proud of my reaction, but that's where I was—stuck.

I thought I wanted to love and forgive, to set aside my own restraints and expectations, but somehow, when it came right down to letting Howard "go free," I dragged my heels. Sure, I could say the words, "I forgive you," but inside I kept waving a flag of rightness over my heart. And nothing moved past this obstacle.

Talk about ambivalence! A part of me yearned to walk up to a chalkboard list of Howard's failings, pick up an eraser, and rub out everything with delighted abandon.

But another part of me wanted to negotiate, remind him of my needs, and then make a deal.

I can't count the times Marilyn and Dick told me, "What leaves a heart reaches a heart." That profound little axiom was certainly true in this instance. For my words to Howard may have sounded all right, but when forgiveness is as measured and reluctant as mine was, the true feelings overrule what is said every time.

The harder I tried, the more I seemed to fail. Instead of swimming downstream in the River of Forgiveness, I was trapped in a lagoon, paddling in circles with no outlet in sight. I needed rescuing!

But no white knight rode triumphantly into my kitchen that day as I sat reading the Scripture that had corralled me with its clarity. No chariot descended from the sky to whisk me away from my disturbing dilemma. Yet, help did come via a verse in John's Gospel. At last, the antidote for my poverty of spirit. Listen to it:

167

"This is the work of God, that you believe in Him whom He has sent" (John 6:29 NAS).

We often interpret this verse to mean it is our effort that brings us to a place of belief. When in fact it is always the work of God that produces faith. One day the emphasis for me was on the first portion of that scripture: *"This is the work of God,* that you believe in Him whom He has sent."

The difference in emphasis opened my eyes to a whole new understanding of how God undertakes for us. Our entire walk with Him is because of a work of God. Our belief, our faith, forgiveness of others—it is all possible only because God is working in our hearts.

Where had I been all my life? Why had I thought I could produce anything on my own that didn't have the shape of some kind of condition? I could no more manufacture forgiveness that would touch Howard at the heart level than I could create a prize-winning rose bush.

God alone could do the work. He was the source.

He who offered the living water to the Samaritan woman would do it again for this woman who, despite all her study, had flunked Basic Forgiveness.

You can't give away something you don't have, something that's not in your heart. But I sure gave it a good try. I knew I ought to forgive Howard. Yet all I did when I had tried to forgive him was what our pastor calls "energize the flesh," more like spinning your wheels in snow. You wear down your tires and you go nowhere.

GOD AT WORK

One afternoon in counseling, Dick posed a hard question about my relationship with Howard. "Jane, why do you continually go back to his behavior? Why can't you let go and forgive him completely?"

I knew immediately what Dick was talking about, but I

couldn't give him an answer. I didn't know why my attempts floundered, why unconditional forgiveness was not flowing out of me for Howard.

Dick pressed in with another approach. "Okay, then let's talk about your relationship with your father."

That was easy. I could answer without a second thought. "We were very close. Like two peas in a pod. I always respected him as a man of God."

Dick wanted a fuller picture. "Do you ever remember a time when you hopped up in his lap and he gave you hugs and kisses?"

I scrambled for a memory, for an instance I could remember. But there was none. Thick silence fell over the table as the true picture of my relationship with Dad dawned on me. I couldn't recall times like Dick was describing. All I could remember was that there was never time for hugging and kissing. Reality flashed into focus like I'd never seen it before.

Dick broke the silence with his matter-of-fact statement. "Jane, you have some very strong feelings toward your dad. Negative ones."

"Negative feelings?" My mind drew a blank. The only feelings I was aware of were ones of admiration and esteem for Dad as a man of God. "No, I protested, "I really loved him."

"Well, if you really want to be released from the emotional pain and unforgiveness you're carrying, you'll need to identify these feelings. In the next few days, if some old memories start surfacing, just start talking about them. I'm sure Howard will listen."

Marilyn added her encouragement to this assignment. "Talking doesn't create feelings, Jane. The feelings are already there. But talking will help bring them to the surface so you can deal with them."

Marriage and family counselor H. Norman Wright sheds light on the impact fathers have on daughters. "Like it or not—your father has made a lasting impression on you. Whether he was close or distant, present or absent, cold or warm, loving or abusive, your father has left his mark on you. Your father is still influencing your life today—probably more than you realize."[5]

Sure enough. One evening a few days later, an old memory of my dad came to mind. Nothing overwhelming, but tangible enough that I knew it was a point to move on. I asked Howard if he'd come upstairs because I needed to talk about something important and I needed him to listen.

We went into the den. I sat in my rocking chair, gently pushing my feet back and forth against the floor, enough to sustain the movement of the big chair. Howard perched on the blue day bed, tapping his foot lightly on the rug. I started talking and as I did, real feelings cut loose from their moorings like ships blown helplessly out to sea. My voice wavered as I described a painful childhood memory.

Howard, who at this point was uncomfortable when feelings were shared, immediately began fidgeting with a book lying on the bed, flipping it nervously open and shut and doodling with his fingers across the cover.

He's not interested. My old instant reaction surged to the fore. He coughed, then cleared his throat, and rubbed his arm as if looking for a tight muscle to massage. Clear signals to me. I vacillated between knowing I should keep talking to touch the depth of the struggle within me and the old belief that I should be quiet because no one really had time to listen to what I had to say anyway.

Finally, I stopped in mid sentence. "Howard, I feel like you're not even interested in what I'm saying."

"Oh, for crying out loud, I'm tired of being picked at for every little thing." Angry, his face turned red and he moved to leave the room.

I stood up, tight and stiff. My face, too, was warming with anger. Tears rolling down my cheeks, I raised my voice to answer back. "That's just how it is with men. They really don't care about women and children." Still louder I finished my attack. "They can't give them the time of day." Now overcome in full blown sobs, I sank back into the rocking chair and let the floodgates open.

Someone observing our scene from the outside would hardly have given us a gold star for our attitudes. Raised voices, tears, and stormy exits from a room are hardly the ingredients of a happy weekend—unless. . . .

Unless the observer perchance knew something about the resurrected power of the Lord Jesus. How He dispatches the Holy Spirit, with infinite accuracy, to focus directly on the depths of our wounded spirits and pain-clogged hearts to open us for His loving, tender healing and allow His forgiveness to do its work.

The vow I'd made as a child, "that no man would ever hurt me like my dad hurt my mother" came echoing back to my remembrance. I heard my own voice repeat the judgment I'd made against all men.

Including Howard.

10

...

Mercy Triumphs

A vow made in childhood. Who would have guessed that a statement blurted out in hurt and anger could lodge in one's belief system and silently sabotage relationships years later? I certainly wouldn't have.

Yet it happened to me.

When I said those strong words: "No man will ever hurt me like Dad hurt Mother," it was as if I immediately donned dark glasses and from that moment on viewed all men from my own injured perspective.

Out of my hurt and anger, I had made a judgment against men. Howard, of course, took the brunt of it. In a sense, I'd imprisoned him, locked him up by the long-standing conviction I held toward men.

Now, at last I genuinely wanted to make things right

with Howard. I wanted our relationship to be warm and open, yet I somehow could not seem to forgive him at a heart level.

Little did I know that every time I drove down the road to Forgiveness—even with the best of intentions—there was an unseen boulder blocking my way: my childhood judgment wouldn't let me pass through. Try as I might to move ahead, the judgment I'd made years before stopped me every time.

I began to see myself a failure as a forgiver. "I seem stuck at this same place, unable to really forgive Howard," I sighed one afternoon as I sat around Dick's and Marilyn's table.

Dick nodded knowingly. "I understand how you feel. It's like a man trying to buy a $400 suit with $10 in his pocket."

He continued with specific help. "Jane, let the Word of God speak to you." Leaning back in his chair, Dick slowly and deliberately began quoting from a passage in Luke's gospel:

" 'Be merciful, just as your Father is merciful. Do not judge, and you will not be judged. Do not condemn, and you will not be condemned. Forgive, and you will be forgiven' " (Luke 6:36, 37).

He paused briefly, then added his explanation. "The definition of mercy here is, 'Don't judge. Don't condemn. But forgive.' This is mercy in action. Before you can give mercy and forgiveness to another, you must first apply this principle to your own life."

His words touched me as powerful messengers of hope. I knew I was hearing truth that would ultimately free me. I closed my eyes and nodded in silence, wanting every word to impact my heart.

Dick continued. "Jane, stop judging yourself. Stop condemning yourself and begin accepting God's forgiveness."

Marilyn looked me directly in the eye and beamed unmistakable encouragement. "This is a rich concept, Jane. Let it sink in for a few days."

And it did. Not only in the next few days, but also in the weeks and months to come.

UNDERSTANDING MERCY

For a long time I'd been trying to do the "right thing," trying to forgive Howard. But there was always that unseen boulder in my heart blocking my best efforts.

But God's Word was at work, dismantling all the obstacles in my way.

In order to forgive unconditionally, as the father in Jesus' parable forgave his wayward son, I needed to quit judging myself and to embrace God's approach. And God's approach to forgiveness begins with mercy.

Mercy—that's the front runner of forgiveness.

Often we can have a sentimental picture of mercy. A kind of feeling sorry for oneself or others. But God's definition of mercy is much more pointed toward redemptive action. His mercy doesn't judge or condemn. It sees through the eyes of understanding and compassion. It forgives.

Let me tell you a little story that beautifully illustrates mercy:

He was just a little boy whose mother took him to church every Sunday. Week after week, face scrubbed, hair slicked in place, he sat stiffly in the hard pew next to her. For him it was only a matter of routine, a duty, a habit, a have-to.

If this was God's house, he thought, why wasn't God home? The little boy couldn't connect with a God who seemed as far away and as uncaring as his sea captain father. Nor could he connect with a Jesus whom he saw in life-size statuary at several points around the church.

None of it made any sense to him. None of it touched him. Nothing registered. Well, almost nothing.

Every year, just before Easter, he remembered hearing the same incredible sentence: "'Father, forgive them, for they do not know what they do'" (Luke 23:34 NKJV). They were Jesus' dying words from the cross.

The words gripped that young boy's heart. No one but God could forgive like that. That thought never left him. While he tuned out "religion" he could not dismiss the possibility of this kind of love that in the face of death wore the face of forgiveness.

It took years and his own desperate need, but at thirty-four he found his answer: He, too, could know this kind of love—through a relationship with Jesus.

That little boy is now my pastor, Dick Williamson. The one, along with his wife, Marilyn, who patiently brought me to a place where I could see the cross in all its awesome reality: forgiveness wearing the face of mercy.

We see mercy abounding in Jesus' ministry. He encountered people caught in the grip of sin, blaming others, and even hating themselves for their predicament. And His response? He didn't judge them. Instead, He mercifully extended healing and forgiveness.

He was a perfect picture of what the Scripture says in the Book of James: "Mercy triumphs over judgment" (2:13).

LOOKING AT JUDGMENTS

In order to experience mercy and apply it to my life, I had to begin looking at the judgments I'd made. Judgments toward myself and others.

Examine with me for a moment the anatomy of a judgment.

Something or someone hurts us and the pain of that incident wounds our heart. Our natural reaction to pain is anger and this anger forms a hard layer over our pain. Judgments follow and these judgments seal in our pain and anger.

As time passes, with each hurtful experience we have, we add evidence to substantiate the judgments we've made. Sometimes these judgments become all encompassing. We paint all politicians, all reporters, all car salesmen, all teachers, all TV evangelists with the same brush of judgment. Objectivity vanishes. From then on we operate from our base judgment, appraising with, "That's the way they are."

What is a judgment?

• A judgment is an opinion we hold as truth. It is not based on fact for we have no way of knowing another person's heart or the things he has experienced. Even if our judgment were 99.9 percent true, it would still be incomplete and that is why God has said, "You leave the judging to Me."

• Judging is based on what we see. We label others by their outward behavior. She is cold. He is indifferent.

• Judgments cause us to prejudge people: "I just know she won't approve of my choice" or "They aren't going to like me."

• Judgments put others down to make us look or feel better.

• Judgments lack forgiveness or mercy.

• Judgments feed on others' weaknesses or faults.

Judging is cruel. It is a destructive, sinful behavior.

What are the results of judgments?

Because judgments are poisonous, they affect everything they touch, polluting, corrupting, crippling, and finally destroying. They bind people, hampering the work of God in their lives. Families have been ruined by judgments. Churches have been split by them and ministries destroyed by them.

Judgments bring death, not life.

APPLY MERCY, NOT JUDGMENT

Over and over in the New Testament we read instances where Jesus illustrates His heart for mercy. One of my favorites, one already mentioned in this book, is the story of the woman with the alabaster jar recorded in Matthew, Mark, and John.

Recall the scene. Jesus is at a private gathering at the home of Simon, the Leper. Into this little group bursts an uninvited woman with an alabaster bottle of perfume. Oblivious to the indignant reactions of the disciples, she pours her costly perfume over Jesus' head in a gesture of love and admiration.

The disciples immediately label this woman's actions as foolish. According to them, she had wasted the bottle's expensive contents; it should have been sold and the money given to the poor. They missed seeing her motive—loving Jesus—and judged her on the spot.

Not so Jesus. He looked at the heart of this woman who had wet his feet with her tears, kissed them, and poured perfume over them—and he did not judge her for wasting the costly oil. Instead, he commended her lavish love.

Mercy triumphed over judgment.

In another setting, a contemporary one, I also experienced the triumph of mercy over judgment for myself.

It happened with my friend, Georgia. It seemed to me in several discussions we had, she disagreed with me or even countered what I said with another point of view. I felt she was not really open to hearing my heart. Finally one day when this happened again I made a quiet judgment: Georgia always disagrees with me.

With the judgment came a decision: I would no longer try to have a relationship with her. You see, when I made that judgment a barrier came up between us. And that's exactly what judgments do. While in a sense they protect us, at the same time, they keep us from having relationships with others. You cannot have a deep, open relationship with a person you are judging.

I continued being pleasant and friendly with Georgia. On the surface all appeared well until one day when a group of friends were together and everyone began expressing their love and encouragement to her.

She started to cry. "I appreciate your words, but why don't I feel your love?" With tears rolling down her cheeks she looked searchingly at all our faces.

I knew as soon as the words were out of her mouth that I held a piece of this puzzle. At that moment, I had a choice to make; I needed to be honest with her. Could I do it? Or was being right more important to me than having a relationship with her? Was I willing to step over my self-righteousness? Would I continue in my commitment to having open, honest, real relationships?

I moved toward her and reached for her hand. "Georgia, I need to tell you that I judged you and closed my heart to you awhile ago. Because I was hurt, I decided to back away from our relationship. Please forgive me for closing my heart and judging you."

By taking total responsibility for my own action, grace and forgiveness flowed. Georgia didn't know what the wall was; she only felt it. But it came down the moment forgiveness replaced the judgment.

From that day on, love has flowed freely between us.

SEEING WITH NEW EYES

The glorious part of being merciful, of not judging, of

forgiving is that we begin to see with new eyes. Talk about sight for the blind! It was like God's unfolding miracle to me.

Remember my outburst about "all men?" A moment of great release came in the next counseling session after I reported the incident to Dick and Marilyn. We began looking at the vow I'd taken as a young child. I could see clearly, not only the vow but the judgment and the crippling effect it had in my relationship with Howard. I had, in a sense, bound him, because I saw him as a man, like all others, who would hurt me.

We talked briefly about my need to forgive my father and Howard and to release all men from the judgment I had against them. Then Dick said, "Jane, you need to bring this to the Lord." He began leading me through a prayer of forgiveness, and as I spoke, deep pain welled up in me and began surging through me. Deep, deep pain.

I would have to call the experience a "divine exchange." As the excruciating pain was released, a depth of forgiveness such as I have never known swept over me. It was like someone took a gigantic eraser and totally wiped out everything on a huge blackboard and then beckoned billowy waves of compassion to roll in gently over me.

I thought of my mother, my dad, of Howard and I wanted to shout at the top of my lungs: "I understand. I understand. I forgive you." Surely this must be how Jesus feels. I was so in touch with our Lord's compassion, His incredible love that only wants to reach out to us in our need. Nothing in me wanted to withhold forgiveness or mercy.

Within the next week, Mother became ill. Dad had died seven years before and she was alone. Late one night, Howard and I rushed over to her apartment and drove her to the hospital. She sat next to Howard in the front seat and I sat in the back, my arm wrapped across her shoulders. Words of love came pouring spontaneously from my mouth: "Mom, have you any idea how much you've done for me? So many wonderful things. Do you know how much I love you?"

There was no need to spell out the events of the past in specifics. The work in my heart was finished and she could feel my unrestrained love for her.

By the next evening she was gone. And I was a daughter, grieving again at the loss of a parent, but infinitely grateful for what God had done in my heart.

I was also beginning to see Howard with new eyes. Howard, the one I'd judged as uncaring and hard-hearted, began to look like a different person to me. Especially one summer evening.

We were standing on our front porch saying goodbye to our supper company when we heard our cat crying for help. A real wail of distress. "Howard, could you see about the cat? Sounds like it's stuck up in the cedar tree." A cat lover, I couldn't bear the thought of our cat trapped all night, cold and frightened.

Nonchalant, Howard laughed. "Hey, the cat got itself up the tree and it can get itself down. You'll see it on our doorstep tomorrow morning looking for food." I heard him chuckling all the way to the family room where he turned on the TV to catch the late news. *He's cold-hearted.* The old judgment popped back into my mind.

I headed upstairs, crawled wearily into bed, disappointed that Howard didn't care enough to make some kind of rescue effort. Then I heard another noise—a ladder scraping against the side of the house. I sat up in bed, pushed aside the louvered shutter, and peered through the window. There was Howard, out in the midnight air, up the sixteen-foot ladder, leaning his tall frame against the tree and calling, "Here, kitty, kitty." I saw him cradle the terrified cat in his strong arms, inch slowly down the ladder, and pet the trembling creature as he carried her lovingly to the garage. I turned my face to my pillow and let the tears flow. What a tender-hearted man I'm married to. And what a wonderful Father we have who helps us release our judgments and receive His love.

I dried my eyes and sat up to greet Howard when he came trooping in the door and up to bed. "Come here, Howie," I beckoned, gesturing to my side of the bed. As he sat down, I took his hand in mine and said, "I really love you."

In ourselves, we don't have the ability to see with new eyes, even when we try to do the "right thing." It is only the supernatural work of the Holy Spirit that plummets to the depths of our hurt, anger, and pain to dislodge that which blocks our love.

However, when the Spirit does the work, we see as Jesus sees.

FORGIVENESS—THE FOUNDATION FOR CONTINUING RELATIONSHIPS

At the Wednesday Men's Meeting at our church, Howard had shared how he'd had a bad attitude toward Jeff, how for years their relationship was riddled with arguments and judgments, particularly after Jeff had gotten into the drug scene. Now he wanted to have a fresh start with Jeff, but he felt awkward going directly to him and bringing up the past.

"Why not write him a letter? Tell him exactly how you feel. Let him hear your heart." The pastor's words gave him hope and a way to communicate the love he wanted to express to Jeff.

Howard composed three drafts, all outlining Jeff's problems and blaming him for his actions. The wastebasket claimed all of them. The fourth try was a winner—a long two-page single-spaced letter enumerating the ways he had been wrong in his harsh judgments and failure to understand how Jeff was struggling. When he got to the end, he wrote two lines expressing how he had also been hurt by Jeff. In simple words he asked for forgiveness.

The letter reached Jeff a day later. Surprised to be getting a long letter from his dad, Jeff could hardly believe what he was reading, but the words deeply touched him. And their relationship, long stalemated by negative jabs and persistent arguments, was restored. Forgiveness did its work. Mercy triumphed again!

At another point, Howard went to Lisa and asked forgiveness for not showing her the kind of love she needed during her growing up days. Again, owning his own actions, he moved in the grace of Jesus, and she too responded with acceptance and forgiveness.

FORGIVING THE DEBT

It's hard to describe the impact of what was evolving in our marriage and in our family. Everything was changing as walls of self-protection and judgment crumbled around us. However, there was one more wall to go—the Jericho of our marriage.

I'd been at lunch with three long time friends. Over dessert, Marie mentioned that the Lord had spoken to her through the story of the ungrateful servant in Matthew 18. Do you remember that passage where Peter asks Jesus how many times he needs to forgive his brother when he sins against him? The law allowed seven, but Jesus said it was seventy times seven. Limitless.

And then Jesus tells the parable. One man who owes the king ten thousand talents is brought before him, unable to pay. Threatened with the loss of his wife, children, and goods, he pleads for time enough to pay back everything.

Touched by his plight, the merciful master does more than extend the time, he cancels the entire debt for the anxious man.

However, when the debtor is approached by a fellow servant who pleads for mercy over a far lesser debt, he grabs him, chokes him, and demands repayment. He who had received such generous mercy refuses to give any to the next person. And, the master servant turns him in to the jailers to be tortured until the full debt is paid. Jesus concludes with stern words about the cost of unforgiveness: "'This is how My heavenly Father will treat each of you unless you forgive your brother from your heart'" (Matt. 18:35).

I drove home from that luncheon, deeply moved by our discussion of canceling debts. Howard and I had been learning so much about forgiveness, but now I sensed one more step needed to be taken. Not only are we to forgive others for what they did, but we are to forgive them for what we perceive they "owe" us.

I was to forgive Howard for what I believed he owed me—past and present—and release him from any future expectations I might have of him.

The Lord had my attention on this! "Lord, set up the right time to talk with Howard," I prayed.

I realized that although I'd often forgiven Howard for the past, I was still communicating the feeling to him that he could never fully repay what I felt I'd lost. In fact, I'd carried the debt over into the future. So he could never be free.

Later that week, I was working upstairs in my office when Howard came in and sat on the day bed. He'd come to ask my forgiveness for something he'd done. This was the time. I knew I needed to bring up the issue of canceling the debt.

Howard had previously told me that he never felt worthy of being forgiven. And now I saw that although I'd forgiven him for the past and said clearly, "Let's pick up and go on," he had continued to get the feeling from me that he still owed me for the future.

"Howie, I've been holding you responsible for a long time for a debt I felt you owed me. As of this day, I am totally releasing you."

The Lord's presence descended quietly into the room in a way we'd never experienced. We held each other and wept as we prayed. All debt was now canceled.

As far as I was concerned that day the enemy was stripped of his power to wreak havoc in our home and our marriage. For two full days following the canceling of the debt Howard sat in his rocking chair in the family room, utterly drained and too weak to move. He wept quietly as he sat almost immobilized, except for his gentle rocking back and forth in his chair.

Something powerful had happened in the spiritual realm and the Lord was literally touching Howard with his healing power in a new depth of release.

A SPECIAL ROSE

One Saturday afternoon, shortly after the canceling of the debt, we were painting a bedroom and we began to talk about the painful patterns we had set up in our marriage.

We both agreed that our pattern of relating to each other had been negative from the moment we "brought in the baggage" with our marriage vows. I came into marriage with voracious needs for love and acceptance coming from the hurts of my childhood. I came with great expectations that Howard would not only meet my needs, but become the source of life to me.

Howard, on the other hand, came with his own needs

for love and significance. He also came with fears that he couldn't measure up to my expectations. Early in the marriage he felt intimidated by my demands. The more I wanted, the more he backed off emotionally, distancing himself safely at arm's length.

That afternoon, paint brushes in hand, we were able to talk objectively about our relationship as we casually painted around the little room. Howard spoke vulnerably from his heart. He talked about the insecurities he'd struggled with since childhood, the tremendous pressure and disappointments he'd felt at work when we were first married, and how panic gripped him at having the responsibility of a family.

"I guess that all added up to my becoming so unreachable," he said, as he brought his explanation to a close. Honest and straightforward, his words seemed to hang in the air, suspended momentarily for me to fully grasp.

Tears rolled down my cheeks. I put down my brush and reached for a Kleenex. There was nothing to say. I now understood why Howard had become so distant. At last I had heard him with my heart.

Again, in our vulnerability the Holy Spirit's presence tangibly enveloped us, paint brushes and all.

Like the Israelites who marked significant milestones with a memorial stone, we felt as if we needed to mark the end of that painful era in our marriage. We closed down our little decorating project, cleaned up, and headed for the neighborhood nursery.

Our eyes lit simultaneously on a beautiful yellow rose bush. We grinned. We knew we'd found our special rose.

At home, by the side of the house, Howard dug the hole. I brought over the bag of fertilizer and a bucket of water and together we gingerly placed our "memorial stone" into the garden soil, tamping it in tightly around the roots.

Our soil-covered hands met and squeezed over the new plant.

"I can't wait to smell the rose," Howard said, wiping away a tear.

"I can't either, Howie," I added, doing my own planting—a kiss on his forehead.

Howard and I were learning to walk in the truth of God's Word, and this lovely yellow rose would blossom each year to become the tangible symbol that we would no longer be reaping the fruit of foolishness from our ways. Instead God would be producing the fruit of love in us—His way.

11
...

The Journey
to Love

Maybe the book is on your bookshelf, too. My copy is dog-eared, highlighted, well worn. Over the years whenever I reach for Hannah Hurnard's timeless Christian allegory, *Hind's Feet on High Places*, I am reminded that I've not been alone on my journey toward love. I wonder how many others have bent over Hurnard's pages and found—like a mirror—their own reflection as I have. How many others could say with me, "That's my story"?

I can relate so easily to little Much-Afraid, crippled and disfigured, on her winding one-way trek from the Valley of Humiliation to the High Places of her Shepherd. It wasn't a health club billboard or the promise of a long reviving soak in a hot tub that spurred her on through setbacks and successes. It was the dream that on those airy heights, she would finally be whole and free. But best of all, it was the promise that the seed of true love would at last be planted deep in her heart.

In my relationship with God, with Howard, and with others, the Lord used so many ways to bring me back to the same penetrating question he posed to Much-Afraid (alias Jane): "Has Love been planted in your heart?" [1]

And I began to see that in many ways my answer was an echo of my limping storybook friend: "What is growing (in my heart) is a great longing to experience the joy of natural human love and to learn to love supremely one person who will love me in return." [2] But what about love with no return? What about love that just gives and doesn't wait for change? The kind with absolutely no guarantee against heartbreak?

LOVE WITH HOOKS

In our world it seems only right. It seems only fair. *Give to get. Give to get.* So much of what we call love marches to that desperate secret cadence.

Remember Valentine's Day in school? You saved your biggest and best for that Special Person. Then when the final tally came in and you received only a generic penny card from him, a card like everyone else's, you wished you hadn't wasted your best on him. You felt embarrassed, even ashamed that you made yourself so vulnerable.

We so seldom have a clue that the valentine of love we hold out to others carries on the back the fine print of our expectations. We may really think we're being selfless. We might even feel safely justified when our expectations harden into steely demands. ("But he's supposed to meet my needs. He's my husband, isn't he?")

I think we all love with hooks, and I'll tell you why I'm so sure of it. Because like our first parent Adam, our hearts have a reflex bent toward foolishness. In a sense, our hooks are innate, but early they become more polished and acceptable as we grow. Like a stubborn crease that persists even after numerous ironings, our hearts fold again and again around the core belief that we can live life on our own terms and make it work for us. It takes the Holy Spirit to convince us we can't.

Like all of us, I've used countless subtle or not so-subtle ways as I've tried to take people hostage with the hooks of my love. It has happened whenever I've pulled people toward myself for my own purposes and benefit, not for their own good and certainly not for God's.

A hook is a behavior based in a belief and may be expressed in many ways. It may be a look, a feeling, a way of responding or not responding, a deeply buried expectation or a loudly proclaimed demand. For years I "hooked" Howard with my questions, wanting to elicit a particular feeling from him. I wanted him to see my needs—and change.

A lifetime of anxiously shaping and polishing our heart hooks can make us masters at trying to extract from others what we believe we must have to be happy. Sounds pretty calculated, doesn't it? But it becomes second nature and we get to be such pros that we even deceive ourselves.

"Not me," you might say. But think: don't you know the feeling? Your husband doesn't pick up on your well-placed clues that you wanted anniversary roses. Your best friend suddenly stops calling you and starts calling someone else. Your usually supportive boss passes you over and promotes the co-worker you trained. Your teenager stares sullenly at the floor as you talk and shrugs off your affirming hug. Winds of war are blowing. Watch out, the war that the disciple James talked about may suddenly be rumbling inside, threatening to kick into full gear.

War? What war? The Amplified Bible gives us a full description of this "internal" war.

What leads to strife (discord and feuds) and how do conflicts (quarrels and fightings) originate among you? Do they not arise from your sensual desires that are ever warring in your bodily members? You are jealous and covet [what others have] and your desires go unfulfilled; [so] you become murderers. [To hate is to murder as far as your hearts are concerned.] You burn with envy and anger and are not able to obtain [the gratification, the contentment and the happiness that you seek], so you fight and war. You do not have because you do not ask. [Or] you do ask [God for them] and yet fail to receive, because you ask with wrong purpose and evil, selfish motives. Your intention is, [when you get what you desire] to spend it in sensual pleasures (Jas. 4:1-3 TAB).

We want. We need. We thirst. Like the woman at the well wanting to find love, the thirst is legitimate; it's what we reach for to quench it that is often so sadly off the mark.

The James passage pictures again the foolish pursuits and beliefs that drive us. The strife, quarrels, and discord that are the result of our own demands for others to meet our needs. This Scripture clearly shows the turning of our hearts, the spiritual adultery of turning away from God for satisfaction elsewhere.

No one told us. But we begin early, even as little children, thinking that people around us have the potential of filling up the deepest places within us. If only we can convince them to do it.

I think Leah must have known something of that. As I read her story in Genesis 29, I could not help but feel empathy for her second-place status and her desperate attempts to make up for it.

Given deceptively in marriage to Jacob as a substitute for the more beautiful Rachel, Leah must have flinched at seeing the disappointment in her husband's eyes on their wedding morning. Her pain only intensified when Jacob married Rachel and according to Scripture, "he loved Rachel more than Leah" (Gen. 29:30).

Hope flickered in her heart time and time again as God opened her womb. " 'It is because the Lord has seen my misery,' " she explains. And then poignantly adds, " 'Surely my husband will love me now' " (Gen. 29:32).

Then again after giving birth to another son, she voices hope once more: " 'Now at last my husband will become attached to me' " (Gen. 29:34).

She kept hoping, kept trying. How many times did she carry a new son hopefully out into the pale light of morning? How many times did she search for the spark of delight and approval in Jacob's eyes, the tender look he reserved for Rachel alone? She tried so hard and she was so thirsty. Like us she must have been battle weary, trapped by her own hooks in a contest she could never win. That was the same place I was when Dick leaned across the table from me and said, "Jane, why do you want Howard to change?" and, later, I knew the answer: "For me."

Loving with hooks closes us to God and to others. And, what is more, it carries a high price. Our homes and health, our children, and our marriages are the casualties. There must be a better way.

GOD'S WAYS ARE NOT OURS

Movie actor, Burt Reynolds, known in years past for his playboy lifestyle, openly describes his quest for love in a recent newspaper article. He recalls growing up in the

South with the traditional saying: "No man is a man until his father tells him he is." To Burt that meant that someday when he was thirty or forty, his dad, the one he loved and respected and wanted to be loved by, would put his arms around him and say, "You know, you're a man now, and you don't have to do crazy things and get into fistfights and all that to prove you're a man. You don't have to prove anything. You're a man and I love you."

But Burt never got what he yearned for from his father. "We never hugged, we never kissed, we never said, 'I love you.' No, we never cried." Life was lonely without affection and affirmation. "I was desperately looking for someone who'd say, 'You're grown up, and I approve and love you, and you don't have to do these things anymore.' I was lost inside. I couldn't connect. I was incomplete. *I didn't know then what I needed to know.*" (Italics mine).[3]

So many of us have struggled on Burt's same journey to love. Longing to be accepted, looking for love, we set out on our journey using our own road map. We've scrambled up the hills of Love Me and down the valleys of Affirm Me and along the treacherous shoals of Give Me Life to get our needs met apart from God. To get . . . that's always the thrust of human love. That was my thrust for so many years.

Listen to the words of Isaiah. " 'For My thoughts are not your thoughts, neither are your ways My ways,' declares the Lord. 'As the heavens are higher than the earth, so are My ways higher than your ways and My thoughts than your thoughts'" (Isa. 55:8, 9). I needed to know that God's way was 180 degrees from my way. I never sat down at a drawing board, sketched out my approach to life, and said, "Now, Jane, go for it. Win a husband, make a marriage, buy a house and thereby be happy." No, I simply went my own way, to have my needs met on my own terms because I followed the bent of my sinful heart, which is always diametrically opposed to God's ways.

Do you ever do things the hard way? Maybe just by mistake? Howard picked up our regular brand of tea the other day at a warehouse grocery where they sell only in large quantities. Eager for a cup of tea I ripped open the box. Rather than loose tea bags, each one was enclosed in an individual package. I tore open an end only to discover I'd also torn the tea bag inside, spilling out the loose tea. Flipping it over, I noticed a little flap marked "Open here." I'd opened the tea the hard way, my way, and I'd reaped the consequences—all over the floor.

God wants us to do it His way, a way rich beyond our wildest imaginations in its dimensions of love. The admonitions of Scripture, including the Ten Commandments, were never meant to hinder us or to stifle our personalities, but rather to show us the way to live life to the fullest. Jesus used the word *abundant*. "'I have come that they might have life and that they might have it more abundantly'" (John 10:10 KJV). If we want this abundant life that God promises us, we have to go His way.

And when it comes to love, God has called us to walk in a way that is not natural to us. God's way of love is giving, not getting. We think if we can get love then we'll be fulfilled and can have love to give, but this is contrary to God's love.

Our "love" is divisive and filled with strife because it is self-directed; God's love always builds relationships. It has no conditions. Our "love" is careful, guarded, and calculating, protecting our hearts at all costs, while God's love is generous and open. So open that His Son died on the cross, hands nailed open and arms outstretched.

I recently asked the women at a retreat in Texas to give their definition of love. They were quick to respond: caring, compassion, kindness—all good answers.

Then I shared with them my pastor's definition: "Love is openness, honesty, and trust."

For a moment the room was silent. Then faces lit up as the women caught hold of the possibilities of this kind of freedom—a love that risked, a love that made itself vulnerable, a love that asked nothing in return. A love that was more than a feeling; it was a choice.

For little Much-Afraid, the path up the mountain to love often seemed like a backwards route. From the Valley of Humiliation, across the desert, on the shores of loneliness, into the forests of danger and tribulation, through floods and mists. Even enduring silence from the Shepherd Himself. Every inch of the arduous route went against her natural inclination to be safe and secure. And yet, somehow she did not turn back even when she was asked to make the final sacrifice: to pull out the root of her own love, that God's love might be planted in its place. And much to her delight, she discovered that *there is always more grace than suffering.*

CALLED TO AN IMPOSSIBLE TASK

At the invitation of a friend, Carol Greenwood and I flew down to Florida in mid January to concentrate on writing this book. Just as we were getting ready for bed one night, a loud boom thundered through the air and every light in the house went out. We were terrified.

For three long hours we sat in the darkness with only a few flickering candles for light. Finally we dialed 9-1-1. Firemen answered our call and arrived to search the house and set our minds at rest: "It's a transformer knocked out by an electrical storm. Happens all the time around here. Nothing wrong in the house. Might as well relax."

Relax? We wanted the lights on! That night, we had

several ways to deal with the physical darkness. We could accept it, curse it, or even convince ourselves that it really wasn't that dark after all. Still, the one thing we could not do was make it be light. Until the electricity flashed back on, it was going to be dark. We could jiggle plugs, flip switches, even shake the chandelier, but without electricity coursing through the wires, all our efforts would be futile. Making it "be light" was an impossible task.

Jesus, too, it appears has called us to an impossible task. Shortly before His crucifixion, He gave His disciples a new commandment. "Love one another. As I have loved you, so you must love one another. . . . All men will know that you are my disciples, if you love one another" (John 13:34, 35). A new commandment. A new standard of love. Through them! Through us! A foot washing, laying-down-one's-life kind of love. Selfless, servantlike, a love that sings out across the weary, tired world like a heavenly symphony, melting hearts, bringing hope out of despair and life out of death. A love that makes a difference—for eternity.

An impossible task? Yes. Meet Jane Hansen, Total Failure on the love assignment. She tried to flip switches and shake chandeliers in the guise of perfectly cooked meals, beautifully manicured flower beds, and an impeccable house—and she could not get rid of the darkness. She could not graduate with a "Love Degree."

As you've seen, even my best efforts to show love were riddled with selfishness. Foolishness was the rudder of my life, motivating me to seek love on my terms. My heart cried for relationship—the very desire put there by God—but I wanted it for all the wrong reasons. Not to lay down my life for Howard, but to get filled up on his love. And what did God want? Nothing less than those fruitless "best efforts." He wanted the "thing" that stood between Jane and God. He wanted to be *the* source of my love. He wanted nothing to come between our relationship. In a sense, he wanted my "Isaac."

Remember the story? God's command to Abraham was pretty clear: "Then God said, 'Take your son, your only son, Isaac, whom you love, and go to the region of Moriah. Sacrifice him there as a burnt offering on one of the mountains I will tell you about'" (Gen. 22:2).

"But God, Isaac was your idea!" If it had been I, I would have protested loudly. "He represents your promise. Your will. You initiated all this and now you want me to put him on the altar?"

Does this sound heartless and cruel? Unloving?

But, wait. God saw the bigger picture. He saw a man, the one He'd covenanted with to produce descendants as many as the stars in the sky, and this man had begun to wrap his heart and life around a person.

The test at the altar of Moriah was not only about obedience to God, but also about God's desire to keep Abraham's heart solely focused on God Himself. Not a person. Not even a promise, but God.

Our hearts are so easily turned aside. It isn't that we are not to trust God's promises, but when the fulfillment of those promises stands between us and our relationship with God, we are in danger of putting something above loving God. And He wants to be wanted just for Himself.

That, also, was the test for little Much-Afraid. Could she give up her human love for God's love? Ultimately that was my test, too.

I could not love as Jesus called me to any more than I could force electricity through the wires of the Florida house. God was calling me to put all my hopes and dreams of love and marriage on the altar. Such a choice cuts across the fabric of our selfish, sin nature. Death to self and all its demands. For Jesus to establish His way of relationship, the way of love and forgiveness, means death to every human effort or aspiration.

In her book *Adventures in Prayer*, Catherine Marshall writes: "The cult of humanism in our day has trained us to believe that we are quite adequate to be masters of our own destiny."[4] But the truth when it concerns loving like Jesus, forgiving like Jesus, is "'Apart from Me you can do nothing'" (John 15:5). John the Baptist told his followers, "'A man can receive only what is given him from heaven'" (John 3:27). Loving like Jesus? Is it possible? With our love? No.

But, here's the hope: "'What is impossible with men is possible with God'" (Luke 18:27). He has already poured "out His love into our hearts by the Holy Spirit" (Rom. 5:5) and longs to give that love away through us.

ARE WE THERE YET?

Station wagon loaded to the roof with sleeping bags, our tent, food for the weekend, and three super-eager kids crowded in the second seat, the five Hansens set out lumbering down the freeway.

As far as our kids were concerned, we couldn't reach the campsite fast enough. "Are we there yet?" Scott, our youngest and an especially avid camper, asked the question when we'd been on the road less than a half an hour. But the chorus picked up rapidly from then on and continued in ten minute increments. "Hey Dad, how much farther to go? When are we going to get there, huh, Dad?"

Sometimes a bag of potato chips or a box of raisins handed to the second seat bought us a little time and staved off the nonstop questions, momentarily, at least. These were kids who loved camping and they didn't move off track easily. Destination was never far from their minds.

It is never far from believers' minds, either. "Are we

making headway? Getting closer? Arrival soon?" Destination looms pretty high on our list, the place where we can kick off our shoes and relax for the weekend in our spiritual tent by the fast-flowing waters. "How much longer till we're there?" Loving like Jesus? Forgiving like Jesus? When will we make it?

Have you ever noticed, that while the Bible shines its light on the hope of heaven, it doesn't center exclusively on arrival? In fact, over and over it encourages us to move ahead, to press on, not to faint. Even to embrace the path. The Lord values the journey; it is "on the way" that he has opportunity to reveal his presence, to lovingly guide, to strengthen us, to provide what we need. In fact, the psalmist sounds almost like a travel agent waving goodbye to a departing traveler. "Blessed are those whose strength is in You, who have set their hearts on pilgrimage" (Ps. 85:4).

"Are we there yet?"

And where is there? *There* is heaven. As C.S. Lewis has said, the life we know now is only the title page. Yet the now of this earth is where we learn the stuff of loving. In his book *Don't Waste Your Sorrows*, Paul Billheimer states: "It is important to remember that this life is a laboratory, an apprenticeship in which God is teaching His children *agape* love in preparation for rulership."[5] This is not where we arrive; it is where we practice.

Billheimer goes on to quote C.S. Lovett: "Heaven is no place to raise kids."[6] Why? Heaven is not a place where we experience the trials and tests that produce growth. Earth is the place of learning; heaven is an entirely different order.

PRODUCING THE FINISHED PRODUCT

But wait. Are we saying that God stands over us, shaking His head, saying something like: "I wonder if they'll ever make it"? No, not at all. Let me illustrate.

A few years back, Bette, an interior designer friend, agreed to help me redo our master bedroom. We talked initially about colors and the look I wanted. Then a week or so later she appeared, dozens of samples in hand and an expectant look on her face. We went through her bag of samples and finally reached a decision on the look, feel, and color of the new room. She spread everything out on the bed—carpet samples, paint swatches, fabric pieces—stood back with upraised hand, eyed the room, and exuded, "Oh, I just love it. It's beautiful."

I couldn't "see" a thing except an old room in need of help and the contents of her sample bag. "Really?" Half-question, half-apprehension, my weak question disclosed my puzzlement.

"Oh, Jane, when I get a room this far, to me it's as good as finished."

Bette, with her expertise in interior design, already saw the end result. She was confident in her ability to create the finished product. All I saw was walls that needed painting, a floor that needed fresh carpet, and worn furniture that needed replacing. Nothing was changed and certainly not new. Yet, as far as Bette was concerned, once I had selected the interior decorator, counted the cost, and decided to proceed, the result was guaranteed.

How like God, I pondered several days later. The same principle applies. He waits and lets us make the choice, He encourages us to count the cost and waits to be invited into the situation. Once these things "line up" then He, like Bette, can say, "It's as good as finished," fully confident in His ability to bring it forth.

In the New Testament, Abraham is described as a "finished product." Paul writes, "Abraham believed God, and it was credited to him as righteousness" (Rom. 4:3).

Nothing is mentioned of the flaws we read about in the Old Testament. Through it all, God was confident, not in Abraham's ability but in his own to produce a man of God—a "finished product." He can do the same in you and me.

To carry the analogy further, the end result of my decorating project was that others have exclaimed over the beautiful room, the "finished product." Invariably, they ask the same questions: "Was it terribly costly?" And, "Tell me, who was your interior designer?"

LOVE'S EXTRAVAGANCE

An example of God's extravagant love toward us comes from a story told by internationally known Christian author and artist, Joni Eareckson Tada.

"That Ken! So thoughtful." Red roses greeted Joni a week before Valentine's Day, an early gift from her husband, Ken. Roses in the living room arranged in an elegant crystal vase. She loved them.

But there were more.

There were roses in the kitchen, too. And the bathroom counter was graced with one lovely bud. Roses in abundance. Fragrant, gorgeous roses all over the house.

And Joni's next reaction? "This was a bit much. . . . Expensive flowers at that. . . . I was irked. It wasn't that I didn't appreciate his (Ken's) gifts, it's just that nobody but our dog, Scruffy, would be in the house to enjoy the flowers."[7]

Joni would be away on a speaking engagement and Ken would be fishing all weekend. No one in the house to enjoy the beautiful flowers. They'd be wasted. It seemed so extravagant to spend money like this.

Yet, as she thought about the ministry of love, she realized, "Love never thinks in terms of 'how little,' but always in terms of 'how much.'"[8] Ken's own ministry to her was a perfect example: His daily sacrifices of love to fix her wheelchair, wash the dishes, turn her on her side, brew coffee before he left for work. "Loving his wife who cannot rub his back or fold his towels."[9] According to Joni, "Love is extravagant in the price it is willing to pay, profuse, even wasteful in the time it is willing to give, the hardships it is willing to endure, and the strength it is willing to expend."[10]

Has it ever caught your attention how many ways God shows His extravagance? We need look no farther than nature to see his infinite assortment of animal and plant species, of colors, and textures, and forms. His artistry knows no boundaries. Birds on every continent singing different songs, trees in every nation bending under different climates, and geological masses enhancing the terrains of every continent—from towering mountains to deep canyons. A symphony in extravagance playing across the face of this planet, the praises of a Creator whose love keeps giving!

Like Joni, we so often squirm in the presence of such extravagance. I have had to learn to receive compliments and gifts with open hands. But my natural tendency is to think, "I don't deserve this. This is too much." Pure love poured out without a way to reciprocate or without thought of the price tag touches all of us who have so long lived lives that measured out love to "the deserving" or "those who can reciprocate."

How much our Father wants us to receive and enjoy his extravagant love. Remember Joni and the roses? The ones she thought would be wasted on an empty house? Well, they were there waiting for her when she returned from her weekend away. Hear those moments in her own words:

I wheeled through the front door, expecting the musty smell of a closed-up house. But I was in for a surprise. The buds had bloomed. Their fragrance filled the cold, dark rooms. And love was there, brightening our home with its sheer, wasteful extravagance.[11]

A LESSON IN LAVISHNESS

Those present at Simon the Leper's house in Bethany were definitely uncomfortable at what they considered a wasteful display. In fact they were indignant when the woman with the alabaster jar broke it and poured the perfume over Jesus' head. The jar itself was costly and the perfume? No dime store imitation. Likely spikenard, a fragrance costing a year's wages. Spilled over Jesus' head when it could have gone to the poor. That's where it could have done some good!

Rebukes came easily from the mouths of those watching. Not just quiet comments, but harsh words. Except from Jesus. The Recipient of the lavish expression of the woman's love responded with firmness. " 'Leave her alone. She has done a beautiful thing to Me. . . . Whenever the Gospel is preached throughout the world, what she has done will also be told, in memory of her' " (Mk. 14:6, 9).

What was it that so arrested Jesus' attention? Could it have been that her love wore no price tag? For her Lord, she would not count the cost. Even what might have been her "nest egg," her "retirement fund," her security, was nothing in the face of honoring her Lord. And Jesus notes it for all time and all peoples: Here is a picture of the Father's love—right before our eyes.

Paul writes a strong prescription for love in his letter to the Ephesians. "Be imitators of God, therefore, as dearly loved children and live a life of love, just as Christ loved us and gave Himself up for us as a fragrant offering and sacrifice to God" (Eph. 5:1, 2).

Imitators of Christ. That's a hard act to follow. He gave His life. In what ways can that kind of love manifest itself in us?

One way I've been learning came from my experience in counseling. Do you recall how Dick challenged me to lay down my life for Howard? When I protested with the long list of things I'd done, he pointed out that love is not just doing things, it is giving yourself for another person.

Being open becomes the anchor of love. For while homemade pies may well be part of loving, God is after open hearts that will choose to lay down our preference for staying hidden or being right or running from relationships. Love is not just doing things for people, it is giving yourself. Genuine fulfillment comes when you give love. It is a paradox: giving away love is what fills you up.

Radical? Yes. The whole world says, "Protect yourself at all costs. You gain when you get." The godly truth is "When you open yourself to give, you always gain." The more you give, the more you come out of yourself and begin to see the world as the Lord sees it.

TREASURE IN HEAVEN

All is such an inclusive word. All. Everything. There's nothing left. Like when you close out your bank account and the clerk hands you a receipt that could just as well contain the words, "Now your money is all gone." The zero in front of you confirms it. *All* leaves no room for negotiating.

In a societal climate that panders to compromise and half-heartedness, all is an old-fashioned word. It means going overboard. Too far. Only country western music dares to croon something like, "I'm giving you all my life, all my love, all my self. . . ."

Look for a moment at a biblical hall of fame of some folks who found something in their lives that prompted them to give their all. A poor widow comes by the temple's treasury to put in her two copper coins. Jesus commends her in front of those who could outgive her a hundredfold. "'All these people gave their gifts out of their wealth; but she out of her poverty put in all she had to live on'" (Luke 21:4).

The list goes on to include the man who found a treasure in the field, hid it, and sold all he had to buy the field. And the merchant looking for fine pearls, finds one of great value and sells all he has to secure it.

Hannah Hurnard's Much-Afraid, too, came on her journey up the mountain to the *all* of the altar. "Tie me down," she pleaded, afraid still that her own fear might rise up at the last minute and resist the very thing her heart was crying for—to have her self-love all plucked out.

And then there was one who could not give all. In answer to the rich young ruler who inquired of Jesus how he might find eternal life, in essence, Jesus said, "If you want the treasure in heaven, you must sell all." We might have heard Jesus say, "I have to have all of your heart." Then He watched as the man walked sorrowfully away, choosing his lifeless god over the God of life.

What is a treasure? We know that pirates have killed for it. Kings have fought for it. Misers have hoarded it. It is precious. Rare. Valuable. A treasure has inestimable value, so much so, it hooks your heart and you will "sell out" to have it for yourself.

"'For where your treasure is, there your heart will be also'" (Matt. 6:21). Jesus was clear. Not only in definition, but in pointing to action. "'Store for yourselves treasures in heaven'" (Matt. 6:20). Make a choice against the immediate, against the gods of this world with their whining cries for refueling.

Choose relationship with the very Son of God. That's the treasure—Jesus Himself.

There is a price to pay, but there is everything to gain. Love costs. It cost God the sacrifice of his Son.

Sacrifice is almost an anachronism in our day. "Have it all" is the slogan of our hedonistic, materialistic society. Satisfy yourself. Take care of Number One. If it feels good, do it. Is it any wonder this philosophy transfers to relationships and we see tremendous breakdowns in families and relationships?

But godly love can penetrate even the darkness of this world by the face of sacrifice.

I know.

As Howard and I began moving in more honest dimensions in our home, learning to trust each other with our real selves, our feelings, and our secrets, we found ourselves deferring to one another, not in a passive kind of way, but in an open, sacrificial way.

There were times we didn't want to be open, and admit our feelings if they weren't "our best," but love called for that kind of sacrifice, even when it was painful.

There were—and still are—times when our comfort zones beckon us to self-protection to avoid conflict. But again, Jesus' love calls for sacrifice of our own comfort that we might remain open in our relationship. Thank goodness real people have a real Savior!

MAKING THE HONOR ROLL

I have always loved the honor roll of faithful pilgrims in Hebrews, chapter eleven. That stellar list inspires me to keep on my journey. People who gave their "all". . . . By faith Abel, by faith Enoch, by faith Noah, Abraham and on. . . . To this day, I have been encouraged because of their love and faithfulness.

But there have been those in my life who have also enriched and blessed me with their love and faithfulness. You've met them in the pages of my story, seeing their real life strengths and shortcomings. I have always loved my husband and my family, but for many years my own pain closed me to loving them freely enough to forgive their human failings. However, when Jesus heals our broken hearts we see with new eyes of compassion and gratitude. We can truthfully honor them.

"Honor," according to Gary Smalley and John Trent, authors of *The Gift of Honor*, "is a decision we make to place high value, worth, and importance on another person by viewing him or her as a priceless gift and granting him or her a position in our lives worthy of great respect; and love involves putting that decision into action." [12]

I invite you to join me in some moments of honoring these special people.

My dad.

I love looking through our scrapbooks and seeing pictures of him talking to Dr. Tozer or leading a choir. He has given me a rich heritage—everything from appreciation of good music to an insatiable love of God's Word. He has left our family with a beautiful legacy of his love of music—a composition for each of his grandchildren. His sparkling eyes, his quick Irish wit, his heart for God. He's blessed my life beyond words.

My mom.

She was so easy to talk to. And she was fun. From her I learned excellent homemaking skills—how to set a beautiful table, how to give a home the look and feeling of warmth, how to organize, how to make something out of little or nothing. She taught me manners, social graces, how to drive a car, and play the piano. She is someone I miss to this day.

My husband.

Howard has experienced his own heart surgery. Determined to get further help, he went alone to counseling with Dick Williamson. He, too, faced the pain of seeing his flawed heart. To this day, he continues going to our church's Wednesday night men's meeting when Dick teaches them to walk openly and vulnerably with the Lord and others.

Howard has chosen to open his heart to God, to become filled with His love. Even at times when it was scary to him, foreign to his background, he has step by step taken his own journey to love. Like a mustard seed planted in his heart, faith has grown as the Lord promised. I honor the work of the Lord in him and appreciate deeply his love.

Our children.

In these past years with sixty percent of my time spent in traveling, Jeff, Lisa, and Scott have graciously accepted God's call on my life. I have felt their openhandedness, generously sprinkled with loving support. How I love and cherish each one. What joy they continue to give me. Truly, children are "the blessing of the Lord."

My brother Jimmy.

My dearest childhood friend, Jimmy played so caringly with me.

He was the kind of brother who protected his little sister. He took me on wagon rides when I was little and to concerts when I was a teenager. Tragically killed at age twenty-nine, Jimmy had come back to the Lord and at the time of his death was studying for the ministry. To this day I miss our warm, close relationship. But I am deeply grateful for those years we had together.

We are all products of the Fall. There is no perfect upbringing, no perfect family. But God always uses the broken places in our lives to "work for good." In my parents' later years we had many evenings and Sunday afternoons of singing the old hymns of the church standing together around the piano. Of laughing over the dinner table. Of loving each other.

WHEN LOVE MOVES IN

When love moves in, watch out. Things change. Love has brightened Howard's and my home—and our lives—with its powerful, healing dimension.

Sparring and arguing, being right, and retreating. Anger. bitterness, hurt, pain—I knew this intimately for many years, as did Howard. But once you lay down your arms, your expectations, and demands, you're then free to receive what that person has to give you. Love has an open invitation to move in.

God did with us what He did for Joseph, sold into slavery by his brothers: He used what was meant for evil, for good. Out of our pain and hurt, out of our stubborn sinful strategies He brought the healing power of His love and restoration. He wasted nothing.

I welcome you to look in on my life now:

I'm standing in a phone booth in an airport half way across the U.S. on an Aglow trip. Lonely for Howard, I call between plane changes just to hear his voice. It comforts me.

It's after church and Howard and I gather up Jeff and his family and head out for dinner. Now, if there's fighting, it's over who gets to sit on Papa's lap or snuggle in next to Granny Jane.

It's early morning on the Edmonds waterfront. Howard and I are walking along the beach, praying, talking, listening to the harbor wake up.

The surf's pounding in front of the condo on Maui.

Laughing and splashing, we love enjoying the surf together. It's the Fourth of July and the family and friends come for a potluck. Howard's barbecuing on the deck, the kids and grandkids are splashing in the pool. Laughter rings out.

I've just come in from an overseas trip. Howard takes the bags to our room. And I head for the kitchen. Flowers. He's filled a vase with red tulips and a few iris and arranged it on the table. It's a far cry from life in the little red house.

I drove by that place about a month ago. Alone in my car, I stopped for a few minutes, gazing at my "dream house." No longer red, no longer surrounded by immaculate flower beds. Shutters missing, fence needing repair, it looked tired and uncared for.

However, in my mind's eye I could still see that sparkling little house the first day I laid eyes on it. And more, I could recapture the one overwhelming feeling I had then: hope. But it was hope misplaced. Hope that ultimately drained from me just as the water from Jeremiah's broken cisterns drained away.

There in front of the little red house, with the rays of the afternoon sun streaming across my car, I thought about the pain and anguish I'd experienced years ago. I thought about my long journey to love.

I didn't know then what I needed to know. That a love far, far beyond anything I'd ever known could be planted deep in my heart. That God's love would flower in "wasteful extravagance," filling me and sending its fragrance all around me.

Epilogue

Now you know my journey to love.

It has not been an easy one, but well worth every painful step of the way.

I am safe in the knowledge that I am loved and secure, that the Lord of my life walks with me on my continuing journey.

My journey began when I realized in desperation that my life would never change until I looked at my own flawed heart. When I was willing to look at my heart and allow God to do the surgery required, I saw how my reactions to relationships and circumstances were reflecting deep anger, bitterness, and pain that God wanted to root out. I saw, for the first time, the foolishness in my heart that had closed me off to feeling God's full love.

213

Inside a Woman

My journey took me over crevasses of pain so deep in my heart that I could not see bottom. Yet it was vital to my healing that I learned to become vulnerable before God and acknowledge those hurts that caused me to harbor wrong beliefs. As I gingerly walked this new path of openness, yielding to the work of the Holy Spirit in my heart, I realized I had been wrongly blaming others for not making my life what I thought it should be.

That realization took me to the self-protective behavior that—like scar tissue—I'd unknowingly placed over my heart. God taught me that the way to remove that self-protection was through being completely forgiven myself, and completely forgiving others.

Releasing judgments, forgiving those I thought had wronged me, canceling the debt—all of these steps were in God's plan for me to experience the fullness of His love and fellowship. A love without hooks that gives, yet expects nothing in return. The kind of love Jesus modeled for us when He lived and died.

Impossible task, you say? Yes, if we take it on by ourselves. But thank God that His love triumphs and helps us open our hearts so He can do His surgery.

The day I forgave the entire debt with Howard, God's Holy Spirit planted a love in us for each other that we'd never known.

Since then, Howard and I set out on a new journey together. Some of the paths are familiar, well-trodden. Others are new and exciting as the Lord gives us greater understanding of the incredible depth of His love for us. As the only One who knows the way lavishes His love upon us, I turn to Him and hear His words, "Go and do likewise."

Source Notes

INTRODUCTION

1. Dr. Larry Crabb, *Inside Out* (Colorado Springs, CO: NavPress, 1988) p. 25.
2. Ibid., p. 24.

CHAPTER 2

1. David Seamands, *Healing of Damaged Emotions* (Wheaton, IL: Victor Books, 1981) p. 12.

CHAPTER 4

1. A.W. Tozer, *The Pursuit of God* (Harrisburg, PA: Christian Publications Inc. 1948) p. 11.

CHAPTER 5

1. Larry Christianson, *Welcome, Holy Spirit* (Minneapolis, MN: Augsburg Publishing House, 1987) p. 63.
2. Vincent Synan, *In the Latter Days* (Ann Arbor, MI: Servant Books, 1984) p. 54.

CHAPTER 6

1. Dr. Herbert Lockyer, *All the Women of the Bible* (Grand Rapids, MI: Zondervan Publishers, 1988) p. 230.
2. Dr. Lester Sauvage, "Heart of Romance: Can a billion cards be wrong?" (Seattle, WA: *The Seattle Times*, February 12, 1992).
3. Ibid.
4. Ibid.
5. Dr. Larry Crabb, Notes from Institute of Biblical Counseling Seminar.

CHAPTER 7

1. William Barclay, *The Gospel of John* (Philadelphia, PA: Westminster Press 1975) p. 152.
2. Dr. Larry Crabb, *Inside Out* (Colorado Springs, CO: NavPress, 1988) p. 26.
3. Ibid., p. 70.
4. Ibid.

CHAPTER 8

1. A.W. Tozer, *The Best of A.W. Tozer* (Harrisburg, PA: Christian Publications, Inc., 1978) p. 109.
2. Edith Schaeffer, "Keeping the Family Together," *Focus on the Family*, April 1984, p. 3.

3. Ibid.

4. David Seamands, *Healing for Damaged Emotions* (Wheaton, ILL: Victor Books, 1981) p. 102.

5. Ibid.

6. Ibid., p. 103.

7. *The Best of A.W. Tozer*, p. 109.

CHAPTER 9

1. Edith Schaeffer, "Keeping the Family Together," *Focus on the Family*, April 1984, p. 3.

2. Abigail Van Buren, "Dear Abby" (Seattle, WA: *The Seattle Times*, April 26, 1992).

3. Catherine Marshall, *Something More* (New York, NY: McGraw-Hill Book Company, 1974) p. 42.

4. *Spirit-filled Life Bible, New King James Version* (Nashville, TN: Thomas Nelson Publishers, 1991) p. 179.

5. H. Norman Wright, *Always Daddy's Girl* (Ventura, CA: Regal Books, 1989) p.1.

CHAPTER 11

1. Hannah Hurnard, *Hind's Feet on High Places* (London, England: The Olive Press, 1955) p. 15.

2. Ibid., pp. 15-16.

3. Dodtson Rader, "What Love Means," *Parade Magazine*, March 8, 1992.

4. Catherine Marshall, *Adventures in Prayer* (Old Tappan, NJ: Chosen Books, 1975) p. 22.

5. Paul E. Billheimer, *Don't Waste Your Sorrows*, (Minneapolis, MN: Bethany House Publishers, 1977) p. 88.

6. C.S. Lovett quoted in *Don't Waste Your Sorrows*, p. 88.

7. Joni Eareckson Tada, "Wasteful Love" (Chicago, IL: *Moody Monthly*, February 1992) p. 32.

8. Ibid.

9. Ibid.

10. Ibid.

11. Ibid.

12. Gary Smalley and John Trent, *The Gift of Honor*, (Nashville, TN: Thomas Nelson Publishers, 1987) p. 16.

OTHER BOOKS BY AGLOW PUBLICATIONS

Heart Issues

Stanley Baldwin

If I'm Created in God's Image Why Does It Hurt to Look in the Mirror?
A True View of You

Janet Bly

Friends Forever
The Art of Lifetime Relationships

Gloria Chisholm

The Gift of Encouragement
How to be a Warm Shoulder in a Cold World

Michelle Cresse

Beyond Fear
The Quantum Leap to Courageous Living

Jigsaw Families
Solving the Puzzle of Remarriage

Denise George

God's Gentle Whisper

Heather Harpham

Daddy, Where Were You?
Healing for the Father-deprived Daughter

Diana Kruger

Who Says Winners Never Lose?
Profiting from Life's Painful Detours

Pam Ravan	**Sock Hunting and Other Pursuits of the Working Mother**
Patricia Rushford	**Lost in the Money Maze?** How to Find Your Way Through
Marie Sontag	**When Love is Not Perfect** Discover God's Re-parenting Process

General Books

Barbara Cook	**Love and Its Counterfeits**
	Romance A God-given Experience of Beauty and Intimacy
Marion Duckworth	**What's Real Anyway?** Eternal Living in an Everyday World
Irene Endicott	**Grandparenting Redefined** Guidance for Today's Changing Family
Carol Greenwood	**A Rose for Nana** & Other Touches from an Everyday God
Ranelda Mack Hunsicker	**Secrets** Unlocking the Mystery of Intimacy With God

Kathy Collard Miller	**Healing the Angry Heart** A Strategy for Confident Mothering
	Sure Footing in a Shaky World A Woman's Journey to Security
Quin Sherrer	**How to Pray for Your Children**
Quin Sherrer with Ruthanne Garlock	**How to Forgive Your Children**
Joanne Smith and Judy Biggs	**How to Say Goodbye** Working through Personal Grief

We at Aglow Publications encourage you to stop in at your Christian bookstore and pick up these books. If you do not have access to a Christian bookstore, you may order tollfree at 1-800-755-2456.

Inquiries regarding speaking availability and other correspondence may be directed to Jane Hansen at the following address:

Women's Aglow Fellowship Int'l
P.O. Box 1548
Lynnwood, WA 98046-1548